CALIFORNIA CRACKUP

The publisher gratefully acknowledges the
generous support of the Lisa See Endowment
Fund in Southern California History of the
University of California Press Foundation.

CALIFORNIA CRACKUP

*How Reform Broke the Golden State
and How We Can Fix It*

JOE MATHEWS AND MARK PAUL

UNIVERSITY OF CALIFORNIA PRESS

Berkeley   Los Angeles   London

University of California Press, one of the most distinguished
university presses in the United States, enriches lives around the
world by advancing scholarship in the humanities, social sciences,
and natural sciences. Its activities are supported by the UC Press
Foundation and by philanthropic contributions from individuals
and institutions. For more information, visit www.ucpress.edu.

University of California Press
Berkeley and Los Angeles, California

University of California Press, Ltd.
London, England

Library of Congress Cataloging-in-Publication Data

Mathews, Joe, 1973–
    California crackup : how reform broke the Golden State and
how we can fix it / Joe Mathews and Mark Paul.
        p. cm.
    Includes bibliographical references and index.
    ISBN 978-0-520-26852-4 (cloth : alk. paper)
    ISBN 978-0-520-26656-8 (pbk. : alk. paper)
    1. California—Politics and government.   2. Constitutional
history—California.   3. Direct democracy—California.
I. Paul, Mark, 1948–   II. Title.

    JK8716.M38   2010
    320.9794—dc22   2010004469
Manufactured in the United States of America

19 18 17 16 15 14 13 12 11 10
10 9 8 7 6 5 4 3 2

This book is printed on Cascades Enviro 100, a 100% post
consumer waste, recycled, de-inked fiber. FSC recycled certified
and processed chlorine free. It is acid free, Ecologo certified, and
manufactured by BioGas energy.

To Anna, Ben, Mom, and Dad.

To Robin, who makes all good things possible.

CONTENTS

PART II
THE CALIFORNIA FIX

FIGURES

PROLOGUE
OUT OF LUCK

Every Californian who lives along the San Andreas Fault knows the moment. The house shudders, the doors rattle against their jambs, the glasses clink on the kitchen shelves, and the question rides out across the city at the speed of the P wave. Is this, finally, the Big One?

It is the same question Californians are asking themselves about this civic moment. They ask not just because the state is in crisis. California has never been far from crisis but has always found a way out, perhaps accounting for what the philosopher Josiah Royce, writing in 1886, called Californians' "extravagant trust in luck."[1] They are asking the question because, in this moment, it feels like the luck has run out.

As we write, California's unemployment rate has reached 12.5 percent, higher than in any recent recession. A few days before the jobs report, the University of California announced it was raising tuition by 32 percent for higher-income students. Angry students, fearful that they would be priced out of their college dreams, demonstrated and occupied buildings on campuses around the state, and dozens were arrested. Frail elderly and disabled persons found themselves unable to hire caregivers because of budget cuts and bureaucratic confusion in the in-home services program. A task force of business leaders in San Diego recommended that the city declare bankruptcy if it could not agree on a package of steep spending cuts and tax increases. The Legislative Analyst's Office released its long-term state budget projection, which forecast annual deficits of $20 billion—roughly equivalent to what California spends on prisons and higher education combined—for years to come. In a six-week period, more than forty initiative proposals were filed at the attorney general's office for the 2010 elections.

The civic moment is defined by more than bad news. What makes this moment seem different—makes it feel like what Californians call "earthquake weather"—is that California seems unable to talk about the crisis in a way that gets to the bottom of things and points toward a better day. The crisis struck the state at the beginning of the campaign to elect the next governor. But in its early months, at least, the campaign offered little of the honest conversation the state needs. The candidates were all "longtime establishment insiders in business, politics or both," wrote Jerry Roberts and Phil Trounstine, two of the state's savviest and most experienced political journalists. "They are campaigning on shopworn rhetoric, threadbare ideology and conventional ideas, offering scant inspiration to alienated voters and angry citizens distrustful and disgusted with the Capitol's ossified operations."[2] At the heart of the civic moment is the fear that California lacks even a language, and an understanding, equal to its calamity.

This book is meant to fill that need. It comes in two parts.

The first part tells the story of how California built and broke its government, sometimes in the same gesture. Others have told pieces of this story, often in greater detail, and in ways that illuminated the meaning of California, both to itself and to America. We stand, in particular, on the shoulders of the great journalists Carey McWilliams and Peter Schrag. McWilliams, writing in 1949, as California emerged as an economic powerhouse and beacon of a better life, showed how California had been "the Great Exception" in the pattern of U.S. history;[3] Schrag, writing in 1998, told how that beacon, powered by the public investments of the Earl Warren and Pat Brown era, was dimmed by the tax revolt and the initiative explosion in the last quarter of the twentieth century.[4] Our own narrative serves a narrower purpose: to trace the string of improvisations and hasty reforms that has given California a governing system both unintended and unworkable. It is meant to present a usable past that points Californians toward understanding what went wrong, so that it might be fixed.

The second part of the book puts forward our ideas for repairing California. It sketches the elements of a new, more democratic operating system, designed to work as an integrated whole. Readers aching for their own policy views to be confirmed will be disappointed. California needs policy solutions for its many problems. But what makes this civic moment so fateful is not just the policy choices California has or has not made. It is that the governing system does not easily permit any firm choices.

Our method has been to stand above the political fray—high enough to be out of earshot of the empty spin and consultant-speak that dominate political talk and the media, but not so high, we hope, as to lose sight of how politics works (and could work better). Our concern is not to advance the policy preferences of the left or the right. It is to re-imagine government in a way that lets Californians debate their choices, settle on the best ones, hold elected officials accountable for results, and choose anew if something doesn't work or the world changes. Like anyone else, we have preferences about what policy ideas we would like to see win or lose. But the task we have set ourselves here is to rewrite the rules to make the game better and fairer for everyone, so California might be governable again for whatever team and agenda voters democratically choose.

The civic moment in California is dire, but it is not unfamiliar to Americans. There was another such time: Government wallowed in debt. Plans to fund that debt foundered on the requirement that the needed taxes be approved in a supermajority vote. Lawmakers bent far in the direction of giving voters what they wanted, but the people remained frustrated that they were taxed too much for governments that delivered not enough. Businessmen dependent on international markets for sales and capital decried a business climate hostile to new investment. Essayists and orators found the system at once too attentive to the popular will and yet not democratic enough.

This time was, in historian Jack Rakove's words, "the Madisonian moment"—the mid-1780s, from which the U.S. Constitution was born.[5]

The men who wrote it, as each new generation of historians delights in rediscovering, were not angels but practical politicians, many with great fortunes they were keen to protect and advance. But they understood that the stakes were larger than their personal interests. "It was more than probable we were now digesting a plan which in its operation will decide forever the fate of Republican Govt.," James Madison told the Philadelphia constitutional convention in the summer of 1787.[6] That plan embodied elements now considered to be liberal (a stronger central government with the power to tax, regulate commerce, and preempt state economic policy-making) in the service of a goal commonly seen to be conservative (the protection of property). The Constitution was not perfect; having failed to confront the evil of slavery, it would provide no answer in the crisis that led to civil war three score and fourteen years later. The government it created now creaks when Americans ask it to meet their needs in the speeded-up world they inhabit. For all those shortcomings, however, few doubt that the Founding Fathers, as they were once called, rose to meet their moment.

This book too is the work of fathers, though not of the kind who merit uppercasing of the title. Between us we have three sons, ranging in age from toddler to undergraduate, all California born. As vexing as California's civic moment is for us, it is critical for them. They will live the history our actions—or failure to act—set in motion. All parents feel the obligation to make the right choices for their children, to be equal to the moment when trouble shows up, in public life as well as private. But because these choices cannot always be correct (a reality our sons will appreciate long before they read it here), the best any father or mother can hope is to usher their children into a world with the tools to make their own choices and futures.

As storytellers and explainers, the best tool we can offer, to them and to other vexed parents, is a narrative and a language to understand California's crisis; a set of ideas to meet it; and our optimism that, if not our children, then some other sons and daughters of California will rise to the moment and put an end to the California calamity.

PART I
BUILDING AND BREAKING CALIFORNIA

1

CRISIS WITHOUT EXIT

What's the worst thing about California's current fix?

The worst thing is not the decline in its once great public schools. It's not the tuition hikes at state universities that make college unaffordable for too many. It's not the cuts to health programs and parks and local governments. And it's not the decaying state water system. Nor is it that the prisons are so overcrowded and unhealthy that the federal courts have stepped in to oversee them. It's not the endless cycle of elections that never seems to leave time for governance. It's not the billions in borrowing that will hurt future generations, and it's not the billions more in retiree pension and health benefits that there's no money to pay for. It's not the joblessness or the lagging economic growth or the big declines in tax revenues (other states, after all, share these problems, if not on California's scale). And it's not even the multi-billion-dollar state budget deficits that persist, and the never-ending cycles of budget cuts that ensue.

No. The worst thing about California's fix is that, under the state's current system of government, these problems can't be fixed.

THE COLLAPSE OF TRUST

Californians know the system is not working. As state government hurtled toward insolvency in mid-2009, voter approval of the legislature's performance fell to the lowest level in the nearly three decades the Field Poll has been taking such soundings. Although voter regard for public institutions and public officials tends to track the health of the economy, there is more to the current dissatisfaction with the California legislature than unhappiness over the state paying bills with IOUs. The 2009 approval rating for the legislature, in which Democrats, Republicans, and independents showed striking agreement, was lower by half than in any previous state fiscal crisis. Voters don't trust the executive branch; polls showed the governor, a popular movie star elected twice by big margins, with an approval rating of less than 30 percent. Roughly four in five state residents told pollsters their state is on the wrong track. Seventy-three percent of those surveyed by the Public Policy Institute of California in 2009 said the state was run by a few big interests looking out for themselves. Californians, always a cynical lot, had never been more cynical.

Gale Kaufman, a longtime political consultant to Democrats and labor unions, conducted extensive focus groups in the fall of 2009 and found that Californians "are as frustrated as they have ever been. . . . A huge amount of disappointment, but it isn't anger, it isn't 'throw the bums out . . .' One woman said, 'It's beyond anger.' There's a level of frustration—they just watch what's going on and it doesn't seem like anything they do makes it better at all."[1]

The trouble for the state is that extreme frustration has not produced any sense of common purpose. The same surveys that document their frustration show that Californians are unsure how to fix their state. Nearly every reform idea has less than majority support. Californians have a long list of problems they want addressed—schools, health care, transportation, taxes, government spending, pensions—but they hold to no clear consensus on what to do about them. "Everybody knows what's wrong," said Phil Isenberg, a former Democratic legislative leader and Sacramento mayor. "But nobody can decide what right is."[2]

WHAT WOULD A VISITOR SAY?

Maybe we Californians have such a hard time figuring out how to fix the state because we are too close to the problem. How might an analyst sent here from another world—think of him as an extraterrestrial Alexis de Tocqueville, well-read in California history and deeply versed on political practices elsewhere on this globe—diagnose California's ailments?

Like many homegrown seers, he would surely note California's polarization. This is no longer Earl Warren's California of the 1940s or Pat Brown's California of the early 1960s, when liberals were sometimes Republicans and conservatives were often Democrats. Californians have swung their partisan identities more in line with their ideological preferences and clumped themselves into communities of the like-minded, creating a new political geography, with a solid Pacific sea of Democratic blue lapping a Republican red inland of valleys and mountains. But our analyst would be quick to remember that the same polarization has occurred in states across the nation without producing the same governing paralysis that besets California.

So he would look deeper, to factors unique to California. He would see that California has outgrown its inherited political institutions, from its legislature to its election system. Its population, now more than 38 million, has soared fortyfold since the 1879 constitutional convention molded state government into its current shape; sixteenfold since Hiram Johnson gave birth to the initiative process in 1911; twofold since the last major constitutional revision in the 1960s. He would also note the century-and-a-half-long flood of immigrants to the state, from all corners of the nation and earth, who turned California into a society of unrivaled human variety. These demographic upheavals have distanced representatives in Sacramento from the represented and strained the ability of old institutions like the state's tiny legislature to accurately reflect the richness of California's tapestry.[3]

On closer examination, though, he would note a more troubling malady: the problem is not one of the body but of the brain. Californians suffer from a deep political schizophrenia.

The extraterrestrial would see that California is governed not by one system but by three.

On the one hand, he would see a system of single-member legislative districts elected by plurality. This structure is well known to restrict representation to the two major parties, exaggerate the majority party's strength, empower the ideological bases in each party, and render the votes of millions of Californians essentially moot in most legislative elections. The system's driving principle? Create a majority and let it rule.

On the other hand, he would see, superimposed on the first system, a second political system: a constitutional web of rules requiring supermajority legislative agreement about the very subjects—spending and taxes—over which the parties and the electorate are most polarized. The driving principle of this second system? Do nothing important without broad consensus. In practice, let the minority rule.

And then on the third hand (here's where you need an extraterrestrial Tocqueville), he would see that, in response to gridlock, voters have repeatedly used the initiative process, another majoritarian institution, to override the consensus principle, which was itself put in place to check the majority-rule principle.

The collision of these three systems and two contradictory governing principles—one majoritarian, one so focused on consensus that it amounts to minority rule—has produced gridlock, rising debt, and political schizophrenia. And that in turn has led to all the expected symptoms in California, including apathy, delusions, disordered thinking, and the citizen anger seen in polls and Kaufman's focus groups.

California has become a place of paradoxes. The state's politics are the most explicitly democratic of any state, but too much of the government seems beyond the reach of democracy. California literally teems with governments—there are thousands, from the state to the cities and counties and water districts—but in practice the state often feels ungoverned. California's system, with its hundreds of commissions and agencies, gives authority and power to so many people that it is never quite clear who is in charge. And the governing system has so many different structures that, to the citizen who wishes to engage it and to the shrinking news media that seek to report on it and explain it, it seems to be without shape.

California doesn't work because it can't work.

THE NEW HOMEGROWN MAJORITY

California's government has *never* quite worked. It had no Founding Fathers. It had miners who rushed here and made a state suddenly, in less than a year. The California they created had no settled system of government. It was an improvisation, a hastily constituted mishmash of Iowa's state constitution and American, Mexican, and Spanish law. The system was unsettled at the beginning. It is unsettled now.

In generation after generation, this has not mattered all that much. California has not had to solve its problems because it could outgrow them. Before it had to reckon with its busts, the next boom would deliver new wealth and new residents. Throughout its history, huge majorities of Californians were born somewhere else. Transplants from the rest of the country and from around the world would arrive so fast that by the time anyone bothered to suggest how to fix the state, California had become a larger, newer, and richer state. It was a place defined by its arrivals.

Being a state of arrival has, in turn, warped California's political talk, long marked by anxious narratives of comings and goings. California gazes at itself in the mirror and worries about its attractiveness: will they keep coming (or might they even leave)? In 1878, when Californians first dared to think about regulating and taxing the railroads, opponents warned that, if such measures passed, "we should be shunned by all the world. The emigrant would avoid us. Capital would keep away from us."[4] In that tradition, the *Sacramento Bee* in 2009 breathlessly reported that, from 2004 through 2007, 275,000 people left California for "the old Dust Bowl states of Oklahoma and Texas," twice as many as went the other way.[5] Legislative Republicans held a 2009 hearing in Reno to show-case former California business owners who said they had been driven to Nevada by a hostile business climate. In worse economic shape than California, Nevada was no doubt grateful for the free publicity.

Yet even while doubting its own charms, California has regularly worried that, in the words of the infamous Pete Wilson gubernatorial campaign ad of 1994, with its shadowy images of unauthorized immigrants dashing through traffic at the border, "They keep coming." In his famous 1868 essay "What the Railroad Will Bring Us," Henry George weighed the price of opening California to the world: "Would we esteem ourselves gainers if New York, ruled and robbed by thieves, loafers and brothelkeepers; nursing a race of savages fiercer and meaner than any who ever shrieked a war-whoop on the plains; could be set down on our bay tomorrow?"[6] During the Depression, the Los Angeles police chief sent 125 cops to the Oregon and Arizona borders to set up a "bum blockade" to keep out the "indigent influx." The Chamber of Commerce wrung its hands over the "horde of undesirables" migrating to the state: "200,000 are here—more keep coming—they'll soon be voters—what can we do?"[7] Throw in a reference to "illegals" and "anchor babies" and you have a ready-made tweet fit for any conservative Twitter stream.

These familiar narratives belong to a California that no longer exists. The state's population still grows by more than 400,000 new residents each year. But net migration from other states and from overseas, once the main source of California's growth, now accounts for less than one quarter of new residents (an average of about 102,000 in the first decade of this century; twenty years ago, in the late eighties, annual net migration topped out at about 370,000). Today most new Californians arrive by way of the maternity ward. The vast majority of the annual increase comes from what demographers call "natural increase," the difference between births and deaths, a figure that has averaged more than 320,000 in recent years.[8]

As a "magnet" for people across the country, California now ranks in the bottom half of states.[9] And its percentage of migrants—people from both other states and other countries—has declined. In 1970 some 76.5 percent of California adults over the age of 25 were from somewhere else;

in 2007 the percentage had declined to 63.5 percent. This statistic, called "lifetime migration," is one measure of a state's ability to attract and retain outsiders. The only state to see a greater decline in its percentage of migrants over the past four decades? Michigan.[10]

If California is less attractive to migrants, it maintains a stronger hold than ever over its natives. Only half of American adults over the age of 25 resided in their state of birth in 2007. But two-thirds of California natives live in California. This loyalty is particularly strong among California's native-born Latinos and Asians, more than 80 percent of whom remain residents of the state. Only four other states—Georgia, North Carolina, Texas, and Wisconsin—can boast of greater loyalty among their native born.[11]

If these trends hold, by the year 2040 a majority of California's middle-aged citizens will be native to the state. Or, as the demographer Dowell Myers has written, California is in the midst of a "surprising transformation" from "a migration magnet that supplies its needs from outside the state to a more self-contained society that depends on its present members. We have become a land of settled and increasingly committed residents who share a future together."[12] Today's teenagers and young adults will form California's first homegrown majority.

This new California is thus more Californian—and more a place apart. This sort of place won't be saved by the arrival of outsiders and the growth they spark. It will need to do a better job of educating its own. It will have to build its own new businesses. And it will need to be a place governed well enough to retain its children, so that they become employers and parents and taxpayers.

California must find some way to govern itself, because, for the first time, Californians must save themselves.

THE NEW REFORMERS

At the end of the first decade of the twenty-first century, Californians of all stripes were proposing schemes that, they said, would save the state.

Leading labor unions and Internet-based progressive groups were organizing ballot initiative campaigns to overturn various limits on tax increases. Businesses were planning measures to undermine those unions' ability to spend politically, and to limit public-employee pensions. Right-wing populists thought that busting the weak if full-time state legislature back to part-time status would prove an elixir for the state's woes.

The riskiest attempt—at once the most promising and the most perilous—came from the Bay Area Council, a policy group backed by businesses such as Google. The council suggested that the state's operating system needed a complete rewrite. In a hastily drafted op-ed for the *San Francisco Chronicle*, the council's president, Jim Wunderman, proposed that a constitutional convention be called for that purpose. But many of these businesses, concerned about the many unknowns in such an ambitious enterprise, declined to give money to ballot initiatives to call such a convention, and the effort was put on hold in February 2010.

The legislature, concerned about all these efforts, convened its own joint committee, the Assembly and Senate Select Committee on Improving State Government, with the goal of holding off the efforts of others by coming up with a few reforms of its own. More than $16 million was committed to a new group called California Forward, a combined project of some of California's wealthiest foundations to produce a series of initiatives for reforming the budget process, elections, and local government.[13]

As this book went to press, it was far from clear whether any of these dozens of proposals would bear fruit. But the attempt—indeed all the reform proposals—had one salutary benefit: the question had been called. How can California cure itself?

NEEDED: A GREAT UNWINDING

Curing California will require more than weak reform medicine administered to address only symptoms. Instead, we must accept the extraterrestrial's diagnosis of systemic failure.

The three conflicting systems must be integrated into one system that is responsive to democratic votes and makes clear who is responsible when things go wrong. The state's single-member, winner-take-all legislative elections must be replaced with votes that provide responsibility and real choice to all citizens. The consensus-based, supermajority-mad rules for making budget and tax decisions must fall in favor of a system that allows for risk-taking, prompt governance, and democratic decision-making in a polarized age. The state's initiative process must be redesigned as a tool to put direct and democratic pressure on elected officials, rather than as a method for circumventing them recklessly.

The whole system must be rethought with an eye to the sheer scale of California, a place grown too large and too various to be successfully governed from the top. Democracy and accountability would be the buzzwords. Windows must be opened so Californians can see in, peer out, and keep an eye on each other. This will require a Great Unwinding of old rules.

In place of a system in which we clamp shackles on a legislature we do not believe to accurately represent our views, and then grow furious at the inevitable gridlock, our Tocqueville would tell us to substitute a system that makes our government more representative and responsive, so the shackles are no longer needed.

Such a new state government would not by itself cure California's worst problems, of education and health care and the economy and prisons and water. But it would fix the worst thing about the worst problems. It would give the state's next generation of improvisers, a homegrown generation at that, enough medicine to have a fighting chance.

2
HISTORY
AND THE CONSTITUTION

The end of the decade was a rotten time in California. Speculative bubbles in real estate and investment had burst. The public had lost confidence in the banks. No one could remember the last time unemployment had been so high in the state. California's infrastructure didn't match the needs of its population. Its prisons were overcrowded. A severe drought was drying up farmers' fields.

This was not the first decade of the twenty-first century but the second half of the nineteenth. It was the morning of March 3, 1879. The 135 men who gathered in the Assembly chamber, inside the state capitol in Sacramento, hailed from a dozen different professions and six different political parties. They had been divided throughout the convention by ideology and geography. On this morning, however, they were united—by the desire to go home. As delegates to California's second constitutional convention, they had agreed to receive pay only for 100 days. This would be day 127 of convention meetings.

Since gathering the previous fall, the delegates had suggested more than five hundred amendments in open session. They had labored over each article of a new constitution in dozens of different committees. But their work had only this morning been assembled into a single document. None of them had reviewed the entire constitution from beginning to end.

The secretary of the convention began to read the delegates' work back to them. The constitution they had approved was long: it ran to twenty-two articles and had hundreds of new, complicated provisions. After a few minutes of listening, the delegates grew restless. They did not want to sit still for a reading that could take most of the day. A motion was made to suspend the reading. It carried overwhelmingly.

Moments later, the delegates voted to adopt the constitution, unread, by a count of 120 to 15. The delegates exchanged farewell gifts, mostly treasured works of literature. James E. Murphy, a delegate from Del Norte County, made an unkind joke about President Rutherford B. Hayes, who had taken office after an election few thought he had honestly won. With that, the convention—California's second and, to date, its last—was over. The delegates were on their way home by lunchtime.[1]

FIVE WAVES
OF CONSTITUTIONAL CHANGE

Such is the history of California's government and constitution. Changes are made, often rapidly and haphazardly, occasioned by spasms of popular anger at the status quo. These amendments often have the quality of hurried improvisations, and they aren't subjected to much scrutiny. The state's would-be reformers rarely have bothered to check their work. And so it isn't long before the reform fails, the popular anger spasms, and another wave of changes comes.

Five such waves have crashed onto California's shores.

First came the hastily scribbled original constitution, drafted at a rogue gathering convened by the military on behalf of a state the U.S. government had failed to recognize. Second were the three decades of failed attempts to put meat on the bones of that first constitution, culminating in the 1878–79 convention, perhaps the greatest civic disaster in the history of a state with a talent for disaster. Third were the sixty years of amendments, more than three hundred of them, nearly all aimed at remedying the consequences, intended and not, of the 1879 disaster. After a break for the Second World War, fourth came the attempt to edit out the worst of those amendments and turn California's amateur government into a professional one. California is now in its fifth wave, a breaker that took off in the 1970s and has still not crested: a tsunami of ballot initiatives that, in the name of putting the fear of public anger in California's professional politicians, threatens the whole enterprise.

Wave following wave. New mess built upon old mess. One disaster toppling the previous disaster. This is California's governing history. The state has changed its system by most of the known methods—at the direction of military authority, by convention, by special commission, by legislative action, by popular vote. Since the 1879 delegates fled Sacramento without bothering to check their work, the constitution has been amended more than five hundred times.

In 1949, when the state was celebrating its centennial, the journalist and lawyer Carey McWilliams focused one chapter of his classic book, *California: The Great Exception,* on the state's penchant for seeking "perilous remedies for present evils." McWilliams's main example? The 1878–79 state constitutional convention.

McWilliams concluded that it was nearly impossible to set timeless rules for a state that grew so fast and so unpredictably. The government of such a place was fated always to be failing, to be running behind. "California, the giant adolescent, has been outgrowing its governmental clothes, now, for a hundred years," McWilliams wrote. "The first state constitution was itself an improvisation; and, from that time to the present, governmental services have lagged far behind population growth. Other states have gone through this phase too, but California has never emerged from it."[2]

California would become a great state anyway. It would rarely have a great government.

A ROGUE GATHERING:
MAKING THE FIRST CONSTITUTION

At first, California had no government at all. In the early days of the Gold Rush, Peter Burnett, who would become the state's first governor, described the predicament: "We have here in our midst a mixed mass of human beings from every part of the wide earth, of different habits, manners, customs and options, all, however, impelled onward by the same feverish desire of fortune-making. But, perfectly anomalous as may be the state of our population, the state of our government is still more unprecedented and alarming. We are in fact without government—a commercial, civilized and wealthy people, without law, order, or system."[3]

California at the time operated under laws that had first been drawn up by Spain and administered by that country's military and the Catholic Church. California's system, with three branches of government that gave special power to mayor-judges known as *alcaldes,* also was a product of the Mexican constitution drafted a decade earlier, in 1837. A visitor to California—in the rare moment when such a person paused long enough from gold mining to ask exactly who was in charge—would have been told: everyone, and no one. It is a measure of the steadiness of California's unsteady personality that the same answer is given to that question today.

In 1848, General Bennett C. Riley, the seventh and last military governor of California, knew that he was not in charge. Congress, consumed by the fight over slavery, was no help. It could not decide on a course for California. So Riley, citing no law and no authority because there was none in such matters, called a convention to figure out what to do. He suggested that some sort of civilian government be drawn up, based on Mexican law.

Ten delegates showed up on Saturday, September 1, 1849, at Colton Hall in Monterey. By the following Monday, twenty-eight delegates were present. Forty-eight people, elected to represent the state's regions, would eventually take part. They were strangers to each other, and in many cases to California. Twelve had been in the state one year or less. Only seven delegates, all Mexicans, had been born in the state. Of these seven, only two spoke English. The original preamble to the new constitution was drafted in Spanish. More than half of the delegates were younger than 40. The oldest was 53. Records say there were fourteen lawyers, eleven farmers, and seven merchants, but at that moment, most of these men were miners, having abandoned their homes and professions to seek their fortunes.

With so little shared history and no existing rivalries, they made decisions quickly and easily. They voted to form a constitution for a state, presuming that the United States would have to let the gold country in sooner or later. They voted overwhelmingly to bar slavery in the new state. They borrowed liberally from a copy of the constitution of Iowa, because it was one of the most recently drafted state constitutions, and also one of the shortest.[4] They argued for a while about the eastern boundary of the state (some wanted to include Mexican lands that are today part of Nevada and Utah) before placing the state line a little east of the Sierra Nevada.[5]

The constitution they wrote was a strange, short, and weak document. It established the basic governmental structure of California: a legislature divided into two houses; an executive branch with power divided up among several elected officials, including an attorney general, a lieutenant governor, and a superintendent of public instruction. It put limits on what the executive branch could do and on how much the legislature could borrow, but neglected to spell out either branch's affirmative duties. Many of its most specific provisions were quickly a dead letter. The constitution declared San Jose "the permanent seat of Government." The constitution said that anyone who participated in duels couldn't hold office or vote, a provision that, if enforced, would have disqualified several of the state's early leaders.

The first California constitution's greatest virtue was that it existed at all. The convention had declared California a state, without probation or conditions, even though Congress had made no decision on the subject. (California even sent two senators to Washington before statehood.) Much of the country thought this presumptuous. President Zachary Taylor complained that California's self-prescribed admission to the union was "irregular."

Glorious as it was to see the people seize power, the new state constitution's serious defects soon became clear. The 1849 convention had failed to design a regime for taxation and government services. A convention subcommittee acknowledged the absence of government services—"We are without public building, Court Houses, jails, roads, bridges, or any internal improvement"—but said it was simply too difficult to collect enough taxes to hire people to collect more taxes. "The smallest amount of taxes, that would justify the appointment of an assessor and collector, would be oppressive to these people already reduced to poverty and . . . in the more recently populated districts, the vast majority of the people have no property to be taxed except the gold they took of the earth and which would be difficult if not impracticable to ready taxation."[6] The committee recommended that the state figure out how to pay for itself sometime later. Maybe the federal government would help.

This was a recipe for disaster—and an early demonstration of the "something for nothing" political culture that would be a constant burden to California. The constitution had provided no clear limits on government spending, on legislative salaries, or on the sale of state property. Governors quickly took to abusing their unlimited pardoning power. Not five years into its history as a state, California's government was broke. "The scoundrels are in power, and they have wrecked the country," Hinton Helper wrote in an early anti-California screed in 1855, after having spent three years reporting on the state. "Today the State is lawless, penniless and powerless."[7]

The constitution, it was decided, was to blame. The legislature proposed calling a second convention three times—in 1859 and 1860, and then again in 1873. Each time, more people voted for a convention than against. But the constitution required that a call for a new convention win a majority of all votes cast, and too many people simply left their ballots blank. Finally, in the midst of another financial panic in 1877, the question of a convention was posed again and the people said yes.

THE GREATEST CIVIC DISASTER—
THE CONVENTION OF 1878–79

The men who gathered at the state capitol in September 1878 were not strangers. They were political rivals. The convention had been advanced by a new organization, the Workingmen's Party, based in San Francisco's growing labor movement. The Workingmen were known as "Kearneyites" because of their leader Denis Kearney, an ex-vigilante who called publicly for "a little judicious hanging" of millionaires and adopted the charming anti-immigrant slogan "The Chinese Must Go!" A demand for anti-Chinese laws was part of a Kearneyite platform that included the eight-hour day, the direct election of U.S. senators, and state regulation of banks.

The rise of the Kearneyites had stirred both parties to combine forces to block them at the convention. Democrats and Republicans, through a joint slate known as the "nonpartisans," had won election to 78 of the 152 original delegate positions. The Kearneyites managed to win fifty-one seats. From its very first day, when nonpartisans loudly objected to the presence of the California governor, who was a member of the Workingmen, the convention was a bitter struggle between the parties.

"There are many distinguished men in this Convention who are more or less warped by party prejudices," said Workingmen's Party delegate Dennis W. Herrington, a lawyer from Santa Clara, during debate over electing a president of the convention. "And I don't pretend that I am wholly devoid of party prejudice, and I admit ... that I have some party feeling, as far as my own party measures are concerned, that would affect the Constitution."[8]

The rules of the convention opened the door to prejudices of all kinds. Small subcommittees of the convention, often dominated by men of similar viewpoints, met to draft the actual language of the new constitution. And each delegate was permitted to propose at least two amendments without interference.

Several of these proposals involved taxes. One hotly debated amendment—a century before the passage of Proposition 13, the famous tax-limitation ballot initiative—would have limited property taxes to no more than forty cents on each hundred dollars in value. But it was defeated by the sound argument of nonpartisan delegate and Sacramento lawyer Henry Edgerton, that property taxes were needed to fund schools and that "it is dangerous to place such matters in a constitution" given that public needs and private wealth can change so quickly.[9]

The nonpartisans, in the manner of California good government advocates before and since, favored high-minded amendments, among them a proposal to bar from office anyone who was so vulgar as to seek said office in any way. The Kearneyites feverishly pushed anti-Chinese restrictions, including one amendment prohibiting Chinese from catching fish, "by hook or net." Peter Joyce, a Kearneyite furniture dealer from San Francisco, in a successful motion to establish an internal convention committee focused entirely on the Chinese, said: "It seems to me, Mr. President, if there is any one thing more than another that deserves the consideration of this Convention, that subject is the Chinese subject."[10]

As the delegates went about the work of drafting a new constitution, the convention quickly became a demonstration of a difficult fact of California political life that endures today: supermajorities are dangerous. The Kearneyites, being in the minority, lost contested votes on convention officers, which required only a simple majority. But on matters related to convention rules and the content of the constitution, approval of two-thirds of the delegates was required. The Kearneyites, by organizing themselves into a solid minority bloc of fifty-one votes, exploited this two-thirds rule to get their way on issue after issue. The Workingmen found they could win by simply opposing the nonpartisans (along with the dozen or so other delegates affiliated with a variety of parties) on every single vote until the majority of delegates surrendered to their particular demands.

The *San Francisco Call*, a newspaper that supported the nonpartisans, complained bitterly about this dynamic in its coverage of the convention: "The Workingmen's Party had 51 solid votes on every question, being well organized. Thus, every day, two thirds of the convention are beaten by one third. . . . The small number wields for good or evil the destinies of the Convention." When pressed on the floor of the convention about this tactic, the Kearneyites pretended they didn't know what was going on. "When gentlemen talk about the minority in the convention," said one Workingmen's Party delegate, "I must confess that I do not know to whom that language is addressed."[11]

The constitution that passed was widely described as a Kearneyite document. It had a few democratic advances. Ownership of property could no longer be a requirement for those who wanted to hold office. Appropriations could no longer be made to private enterprises. Local government was put on a firmer footing, with cities permitted to create their own charters. The courts were reorganized, eschewing the Mexican model and establishing the seven-member state supreme court Californians know today.

But the zeal of the Kearneyites also produced lasting damage to the document—and to the state. They codified their hatred of the Chinese in a whole article of the constitution that, in violation of the U.S. Constitution, prohibited the immigration of Chinese to the state and barred corporations from employing the Chinese. This constitutional provision was not only a racist abomination; it also created a problem for American foreign policy in the Far East for the next half-century.

But it was in matters of corporate regulation that the Workingmen most badly miscalculated. To check the power of the Southern Pacific Railroad, the state's most important corporation, the new constitution established a powerful railroad commission. This body was easily captured by the Southern Pacific itself, through extensive use of bribes. In purpose, the railroad commission was turned on its head, becoming the railroad's primary bureaucratic tool for dominating California's government and raiding its treasury.

The new constitution delivered in March 1879—and narrowly approved by voters that May—proved to be a landmark, though not in a favorable way. Much of the next half-century of political reform efforts in California would be devoted to undoing its worst provisions.

A JURY THAT COULD NOT BE FIXED—
SIXTY YEARS OF AMENDMENTS

The Progressive movement flourished throughout the western United States in the late nineteenth and early twentieth centuries. In California it was an unusually powerful and angry movement, intent on cleansing state government of the influence of the railroad and other baleful interests.

California's Progressives were mostly entrepreneurs and professionals, men who had moved to the state to make a name, a fortune, or both. They distrusted both labor and corporations (at least corporations other than their own). They spoke in the name of "the people" but had little affection for the people's pleasures; Progressives were just as easily to be found at the meeting of the Anti-Saloon League, the Anti-Race Track Gambling League, or the Sunday Rest League as at the Lincoln-Roosevelt League, their statewide organization. Operating outside party structures, they were adept at using the burgeoning newspapers of the state, where some of the most prominent of them were owners or editors, to advance their crusades and build up their candidates. As George Mowry described them in his classic history, California's Progressives took an unusually strong interest in science and pseudo-science, including eugenics and the newly emerging field of public opinion research. Public opinion, the California progressive journalist Lincoln Steffens famously said, was a "jury that could not be fixed."[12]

In that spirit, the Progressives, who saw their ideas routinely blocked in the legislature, seized on the Swiss innovation of direct democracy as central to reforming California. They won victory first in 1903 in Los Angeles, which adopted the initiative (popular votes on creating new laws), referendum (popular votes to reverse legislative acts), and recall (popular votes to remove elected officials mid-term). But in San Francisco, the state's largest town, the Progressives were stymied until the disastrous earthquake and fire of 1906 destroyed the city. No longer willing to tolerate rampant bribery, prominent San Franciscans launched prosecutions of the city's bosses—Mayor Eugene Schmitz and labor leader Abe Ruef.

Those prosecutions, known as the graft trials, galvanized the Progressive movement. Nodding to popular anger, the railroad-bought Democratic and Republican parties agreed to let voters pick their nominees for state-wide offices in 1910 through a direct primary.

Sensing an opening, the Progressives convinced a famous and flamboyant graft-trials prosecutor, Hiram Johnson, who had never before run for office, to seek the Republican nomination for governor. He was a risky choice. A volatile man prone to black moods and even suicidal fantasies, he had exchanged blows with opposing lawyers in the courtroom and called for retributions against jurors if they were to let off the San Francisco labor boss Ruef. (The jury, thus threatened, voted to convict.) In a letter to a friend, Johnson confessed that he did not possess the right temperament for public office.[13]

Improbably, this novice would remake the state's government and politics. A dynamic campaigner skilled at stirring crowds to anger ("Johnson's surely as entertaining as a nickelodeon, and the people didn't have to pay a cent," one rival campaign manager told a San Francisco newspaper),[14] Johnson beat the railroad machine candidates in the 1910 Republican primary, which was the real election in a GOP-dominated state. In his first months in office in 1911, Governor Johnson convinced the legislature to place twenty-three constitutional amendments on the ballot in an October special election.

Taken together, the amendments were as ambitious as the 1878–79 convention. Among these measures were women's suffrage, the establishment of a workers' compensation system, greater autonomy for cities and counties, and new standards for school textbooks and criminal appeals. A new railroad commission was established to replace the old corrupt one. But the three amendments that would contribute most to California's governing system were the direct democratic tools: the initiative, the referendum, and the recall.

The main controversy involved applying the recall to judges, a provision that drew criticism from President Taft, among others. The establishment of the initiative process, which would quickly become central to the conduct of state politics and government, was the subject of almost no debate at all.

Twenty-two of the twenty-three measures won (a measure permitting public officials to ride for free on the railroads lost). The controversial recall received support from 77 percent of voters. The initiative process won 168,744 votes, with only 52,093 against, according to state records.

The success of the 1911 measures touched off a thirty-year public rewrite of the constitution. It started almost immediately. Three referendums and three initiatives qualified for the general election ballot in 1912. In 1914, Californians faced seventeen initiatives. (They voted no on all but five, establishing a pattern of rejecting most direct democratic measures that continues to this day. Proposals to abolish the poll tax, suspend prohibition laws, consolidate cities, regulate prize fights, and sell bonds for the University of California were the winners.) Watching how these tools were actually used soured some Progressives. Johnson himself lost a piece of legislation to the referendum.

"I am quite aware that this year the referendum has been put to some base uses," Johnson told a Sacramento crowd during his 1914 reelection campaign. "I am aware too that the initiative may have been as you would have preferred it should not be used. But I beg you ever to remember that there may again come a time in our state when our old political masters would fasten upon us the old political yoke, and if that time ever again comes in the State of California, the most powerful weapons that you will have for your defense and the perpetuity of what you hold most dear politically, will be the initiative, the referendum and the recall. And so do not condemn a system fraught with such potential possibilities for you because in exceptional instances it may have been used in a fashion with which you disagree."[15]

Johnson was less sanguine after eleven measures he backed—including a referendum on his top priority, making all state elections nonpartisan—were defeated badly in a 1915 special election. ("I am rather fearful that our people are sick of campaigns and probably sick of the campaigner," he confided in a letter to a friend near the end of that unsuccessful campaign, "but I don't know how else to arouse the interest necessary for success.")[16] But frequent defeat did not stop both legislators and the voters themselves from proposing hundreds of new amendments. Among these was an amendment, first suggested by State Controller Ray Riley when California faced a then-record $50 million budget deficit, to require a two-thirds vote to pass appropriations when spending grew by more than 5 percent from one two-year budget to the next. And so with little debate, the two-thirds supermajority was added to a ballot measure approved by voters in November 1933.[17]

By 1940, the 1879 document had been amended 343 times. It ran to more than 65,000 words. In effect, California had a new constitution, its third.

This new document required a government far larger and more complex. Authority was distributed among elected leaders, a large new civil service, and a growing maze of boards and commissions with unelected members. It was nearly impossible for one party or boss to dominate in such a system. It was not easy to govern either. And it would become harder and harder for voters to know whom to hold responsible for problems. Interest groups were already busy using the initiative to protect their pet projects and resist democratic accountability. As V. O. Key and Winston Crouch wrote in 1938 for their study *The Initiative and Referendum in California*, "the groups using the initiative have not differed from the organizations lobbying before the legislature . . . representing interests—commercial, industrial, financial, reform, religious, political."[18]

For all its profound advances, the new Progressive system launched in 1911 also made the state's politics bigger and louder. Debates on big issues played out in the context not of legislative debate but of campaigns. Since ballot initiatives were rarely a product of one particular party or politician, the campaigns could not rely on party managers. So the new constitution helped launch a new class of professional campaign managers. Together, these pros became a permanent and powerful force in the state's governing system, building and preserving a political culture that, in the Progressive tradition, revered public opinion, loathed partisanship and ideology, and encouraged as many campaigns as possible. The *San Diego Union,* worried about direct democracy in 1911, editorialized: "California appears doomed to be continually in the throes of politics. As soon as one election is over, long-range campaigning for the next one will begin. This sort of political endless chain is not alluring." The newspaper was right. But this is the same political culture that prevails in California today.

The political class also made winning, not ideas, its priority, and thus produced a cynical kind of politics that traded in ugliness. Johnson himself made a point of identifying an enemy in each of his campaigns, whether that enemy was the railroad or the unions or, in too many cases, Asian immigrants. As governor, Johnson signed an act barring "aliens" from owning land in the state—despite a personal appeal from the U.S. secretary of state. Voters, via ballot initiative, later tightened these restrictions. Tellingly, one of the few parts of the 1879 constitution not substantially altered during this era was the anti-Chinese article. "In many respects, Johnsonism resembled Kearneyism," Carey McWilliams would write in 1949, "but Johnson was an abler and far more intelligent demagogue than Kearney."[19]

This was a governing system built on contempt—contempt for the dirty side of political deal-making, contempt for power, contempt for politics and politicians, and ultimately contempt for racial and ethnic minorities. Johnson, in thirty-five years of campaigns (he would leave the governorship in 1916 for a U.S. Senate seat he held until his death in 1945), never stopped claiming, as he did in his first race in 1910: "I am not a politician, so I am not trying to pose as one. And that is one reason why I expect to be elected governor. I think, and the people seem to think, that California has been ruled long enough by politicians."[20] One hundred years later, California's politicians are still running for office by saying that politicians have ruled too long.

THE MID-SIXTIES REVISION—
FROM AMATEURS TO PROFESSIONALS

World War II and the postwar period brought change and turmoil to California, but the state constitution remained relatively untouched. It had already been touched enough. California's governing document was the second longest state constitution, after Alabama's. Changing such a monstrosity seemed like too much trouble. "Since 1879, of course," McWilliams wrote in 1949, "all the powerful organizations have gotten their particular pet schemes, their 'sacred cows,' written into the state constitution; so that the adoption of a new state constitution presents a well-nigh insoluble political problem."[21]

Nevertheless, as the state's population and economy grew by leaps and bounds, elites sought to prune California's document and its governing system. A few pieces of the constitution were deleted in a 1949 special election called by Governor Earl Warren. More editing was needed, but the constitution at the time permitted only amendments, not a revision, without a convention. So in 1962, the legislature asked voters to amend the constitution to permit lawmakers to draft revisions and submit them to the people. The legislative measure, Proposition 7, passed in November of that year. The following year, the legislature—declaring that the constitution had grown "to be bad in form, inconsistent in many respects, filled with unnecessary detail, and replete with matter which might more properly be contained in the statutory law of the State"[22]—established the California Constitution Revision Commission.

Composed of sixty volunteer citizen members and six legislators (as well as sixteen ex-officio legislative members), the revision commission focused mainly on removing nonfundamental parts of the constitution and converting them to statutes. Barry Keene, a member of the commission, would recall his clear instructions from legislative leaders: "Avoid anything that steps on important political issues."[23] In all, about 16,000 words were deleted from the document, and seven articles of the documents were substantially revised. Voters approved the revisions in 1966 overwhelmingly, with both candidates for governor—Democratic incumbent Pat Brown and the eventual Republican victor, Ronald Reagan—in support. (Voters would approve further deletions and some technical changes, particularly in rules on local government, in 1970 and 1974.)

Uncontroversial at the time, these changes later would fuel a backlash. The revisions were driven by two contradictory impulses: creating a more professional government while at the same time granting more power to amateurs, mostly through the initiative process.

In the name of creating a more professional legislative branch, the revision commission permitted the legislature, which had been limited to 120-day sessions, to meet full-time. The commission also lifted a requirement that had restricted budget sessions to every other year. The revision mandated new conflict-of-interest statutes; among those produced were restrictions on legislators' expenses and retirement benefits. And the revised constitution permitted the legislature to set its own compensation, provided that increases were no more than 5 percent.

In the name of amateurism, the revision commission opened up the initiative process, slightly, but in ways that would prove profound. The commission formally removed the legislature from having any role in initiatives by deleting the "indirect initiative," a little-used provision that had permitted initiative sponsors to offer their initiatives to the legislature first for action. More seriously, the commission eased the qualifying standards for initiatives that merely changed statutes (as opposed to initiatives that changed the constitution). Previously, initiative sponsors had had to collect a number of valid signatures equal to 8 percent of the number of people who had voted in the most recent gubernatorial election. After the revision, initiative statutes required only 5 percent of gubernatorial voters.

"This was done," explained Orange County Superior Court Judge Bruce W. Sumner, who chaired the commission, "to encourage persons wishing to sponsor initiative petitions to use the initiative statute, thus protecting the Constitution from addition of unnecessary detail."[24] This proved to be a crucial and timely change, though hardly in the way Sumner intended.

The lower standard for initiative statutes would trigger a new wave of initiatives after the relatively empty ballots of the early postwar. In the entire 1940s, just nineteen initiatives were presented to the voters. In the 1950s, only ten initiatives were presented. The 1960s saw nine. What caused the decline? Some surveys of the time suggested that direct democracy had been discredited among a war-scarred generation by the plebiscites of dictators like Hitler, Stalin, and Nasser. California's desire for direct action also may have been tempered by three popular governors: Earl Warren, Goodwin Knight, and Pat Brown.

But a more important barrier to using the initiative, referendum, or recall was the huge surge in the state's population. The standards for qualifying measures for the ballot were based on percentages. A number of signatures equal to 5 percent of the voters in the most recent gubernatorial election was required for a referendum, 8 percent for an initiative, 12 percent for a recall. Before 1940, the state's population had been less than 7 million, and a measure could qualify with as few as 100,000 signatures. By 1970, California had more than 20 million residents. As a result, qualifying an initiative required getting more than half a million signatures—a considerably more complicated and expensive task.

The easing of constitutional requirements for initiatives was quickly followed by legislative and judicial actions that made life easier for initiatives' sponsors. In 1968, two years after voters approved the constitutional revision, the legislature permitted initiatives to appear on the ballot in primary elections; previously, initiatives had been limited to general elections. In 1979 the California Supreme Court ruled that malls are the functional equivalent of town squares, a decision that opened up shopping centers to circulators of initiative petitions and made signature gathering faster and cheaper. The legislature also ended the onerous "precincting" requirement for initiatives. This law had mandated that voters list their exact precinct number next to their signature on initiative petitions. Since few voters could recite their precincts, signature gatherers had to take the extra, time-consuming step of visiting county clerks' offices, looking up the precinct number of each signer, and filling in the numbers by hand. Ending precincting saved signature gatherers a step.

The easing of restrictions on signature gathering coincided with a bit of innovation. Ed Koupal, a failed bar owner from a Sacramento suburb who sponsored various environmental initiatives in the 1970s, invented the "table method" for gathering signatures. He discovered that petition circulators could produce huge volumes of signatures—eighty signatures an hour became the standard—by working in pairs outside a store. One would sit at a table near the entrance with the petition, while the other approached shoppers with a clipboard. Koupal urged his circulators not to waste time talking with people about the issue raised by an initiative. "Don't debate or argue!" Koupal said. "Why try to educate the world when you're trying to get signatures?"[25]

The impact of Koupal's advances, when combined with the newly deregulated signature market, would reshape state politics. In 1972, ten initiatives, on subjects from marijuana legalization to the death penalty, appeared on statewide ballots—a one-year total that surpassed the number of initiatives on the ballot in the previous decade.

The easing of restrictions on initiative petitions provided an opening for California's small but growing movement of anti-tax conservatives. Before the process changed, leading anti-tax activists—including Los Angeles County assessor Phil Watson, Sacramento real estate salesman Paul Gann, and Howard Jarvis, the leader of an association of Southern California apartment building owners—struggled to qualify measures for the ballot. But in late 1977, Watson prodded Jarvis and Gann to combine forces.

The initiative they drafted was ambitious. It proposed to cap property taxes at 1 percent of a property's market value. Absent a sale or major remodeling, the assessed market value of a property could not increase more than 2 percent a year. And while California since 1935 had required a two-thirds vote for the legislature to pass a budget, the initiative extended that two-thirds supermajority rule to any increase in state tax revenue.

Working under the new initiative rules, Jarvis and Gann would easily qualify their initiative, which drew the unlucky number 13. During the campaign, when Jarvis was asked whether a ballot initiative was the best way to make such dramatic changes in California taxes and government, he would reply: "Better government by the masses than government by the asses!"

Proposition 13 would be tested repeatedly over the next thirty years, as voters and lawmakers crafted a post–Prop 13 California in a flurry of initiatives and amendments. This new and ongoing rewrite of the state's governing system—the fifth such wave, after the improvised constitution of 1849, the messy Kearneyite rewrite of 1879, the Progressive amendments of the early twentieth century, and the constitutional revision of the 1960s—would prove no more successful than its predecessors.

3

EMPOWERING AND SHACKLING SACRAMENTO

Throughout the 1960s and 1970s they had been telling their stories at neighborhood coffee klatches and at tax protest rallies, to elected officials and newspaper reporters, to anyone who would listen. They were people like George and Mary, who told their story, minus last names, to the *Los Angeles Times*.

A disabled victim of a car crash, George received about five hundred dollars a month in disability benefits; Mary was laid off when the aerospace plant where she worked closed down. They lived, with their six children, in the one-bedroom Venice house they had bought for $19,500 in 1962, when the property taxes were $221.30 a year. By 1976, when they talked to the *Times*, the taxes had almost quintupled to about $1,100 on a house now worth $32,000, mostly because it could be torn down to make way for one of the apartment houses sprouting near the beach. With the taxes and the mortgage and the food (they were down to one meal a day) and three sons at college, there were only bad choices ahead for them— sell the house or take the boys out of college. All because of the soaring property taxes.[1]

Marilyn Noorda, head of the taxation committee of the Sherman Oaks Homeowners Association, was much better off. Her husband, Glen, a Hollywood union stagehand, made about $24,000 a year, well above the

Los Angeles median of $14,000. But by 1976 the property tax on their three-bedroom home had reached $2,400, almost as much as the annual mortgage, and about one dollar for every seven dollars of Glen Noorda's take-home pay. The next year it would rise to about $3,000.[2]

No one ever intended for property taxes on homes to go so high. It happened inadvertently, the result of one of California's spasms of reform, enacted in the Progressive faith that rules and experts were a better way to run California than politics and politicians' discretion.

THE KINDNESS OF ASSESSORS

It began with Russell Wolden, the tax assessor in San Francisco, fated to be known forever as the "Crooked Assessor." Before Prop 13, county tax assessors mattered. How much a home or business-property owner paid in property taxes turned on two things: the tax rates set by your city, county, and school district, and the value the assessor put on your property. Even if tax rates went down, your tax bill could still go up if the assessor, at his discretion, said your house or factory had increased in value. And vice versa—with the accent on "vice."

Wolden's name hit the headlines in 1965 when a whistleblower revealed that the assessor's discretion was for sale; businesses that paid him for "consulting" services got their assessments lowered. In the following months, investigations around the state turned up more cases of assessors handing out low-ball assessments to businesses that had contributed to their campaigns or stuffed dollars into their pockets. Wolden and several other assessors went to jail, and the San Diego assessor committed suicide.

Even before the Crooked Assessor became news, the Assembly's tax committee had uncovered the assessment racket and put together a far-reaching plan, supported by Speaker Jesse Unruh and Assemblyman Nicholas Petris, a liberal Democrat from Oakland, to overhaul the whole state and local tax system to reduce reliance on the property tax. The plan called the property tax "outmoded, discriminatory, unfair, economically destructive, and regressive," bad in both theory and practice. But this comprehensive approach foundered in 1965. County tax assessors fought to keep their power, and Governor Edmund G. (Pat) Brown didn't want to kick off his reelection campaign by raising state taxes to make up the lost revenue to schools and other local governments if the property tax were reduced and reformed. (Another Governor Brown would soon make a similar calculation, with even greater consequences.)

Instead, in 1966 the legislature and Brown enacted a narrower bill, AB 80. It required all property to be assessed at a standard rate of 25 percent of market value. Gone was the county assessors' discretion. With the papers still reporting on the assessors' trials, California's leaders had promptly answered scandal with reform. But reform begat something entirely unexpected and unintended: soaring property taxes for homeowners.[3]

The newspaper reports about crooked assessors had left out a key piece of the story: homeowners had been the biggest beneficiaries of assessors' discretion.

In the postwar boom, as 10 million Californians became 20 million, assessors up and down the state had been sheltering them from the gale of rising property tax rates. All those new people needed roads and police and parks and teachers and schools. "I don't think that they've built a new schoolhouse in Brooklyn in the last 20 years," the Los Angeles County assessor explained in 1957. "But we've got to build a new one every week."[4] Local elected officials, looking for property tax revenue to pay for those public goods, pushed hard on assessors to produce higher assessments as home prices went up.

But assessors were elected officials too. They did not earn their tickets to reelection or promotion by rapidly raising assessments on voters. They had heard the thousands of working- and middle-class families in the late 1950s and early 1960s who held protest meetings and trooped off to berate their elected officials for rising property taxes. The assessors couldn't provide full relief, but they had leaned against the wind, letting business assessments rise while holding back on full increases for homeowners.

Before AB 80 passed, homeowners in San Francisco were paying taxes on 9 percent of market value and commercial property owners were paying on 35 percent of market value. Los Angeles homeowners were assessed at 21 percent of value and commercial property owners at 45 percent. To protect homeowners (and their own careers), assessors had used their discretion to create an informal split roll, taxing business at a higher rate. By passing AB 80, the legislature had inadvertently repealed that split roll and required local governments to lower taxes on business and shift the property tax burden to homeowners.[5]

In the late sixties and early seventies, with counties sending out the higher assessments triggered by AB 80, grassroots groups of all kinds—seniors and welfare rights organizations, unions, homeowner associations formed to protest development, taxpayer associations—rallied against higher property taxes. Twice initiatives to cut property taxes were qualified for the statewide ballot; each time, in 1968 and 1972, Governor Reagan and the legislature responded with legislation to hold down tax bills. Both initiatives failed.[6]

CALIFORNIA COMES UNHINGED

In the mid-seventies, though, inflation took off in California's real estate market. With the economy booming and people still flocking to live in the sun, home prices jumped by 2 or 3 percent a month. A buying panic set in. Fearful that they would miss a chance to buy if they didn't buy now, people snapped up houses faster than the developers' bulldozers could clear orchards to plant new subdivisions, bidding up prices even more. And because California had put assessment on autopilot, property taxes rode the same upward trajectory, with assessments more than doubling from 1975 to 1978—not just for new buyers but for people who had bought a cheap bungalow decades earlier and now found themselves owning, and paying huge taxes on, a house newly worth far more than they could ever afford to buy on their incomes.[7]

For millions of Californians, it was time of dizzying and unwelcome change, the defeat of their California dreams. Smog filled the sky, traffic choked the freeways, and the radio alternated between Joni Mitchell singing about how they had paved paradise and a newsman breathlessly delivering the latest report on Watergate, lines at the gas pump, or inflation. It made people like Dan Shapiro, president of a San Fernando Valley neighborhood group, think back to what he remembered as a Los Angeles golden age:

> At the end of the day you were in your castle—a back yard filled with fruit trees and a monthly payment of $183, a price most people could afford. . . . Los Angeles was safe. Its police department was among the best in the country. If you needed assistance, it was provided immediately, with courtesy. . . . Schools were good. A young man or woman attending public schools in Los Angeles had as good a chance to attend the best universities as a graduate of any exclusive private school, assuming equal performance. . . .
>
> Then suddenly in the 1970s the city that worked stopped working. . . . Thus we have a city with mediocre schools, poor police protection, planning and transportation in chaos.[8]

Out of this sense that California had come unhinged was born a movement—more Californians were in motion than during Hiram Johnson's day, and more than at any time since. These people were, in many ways, the opposite of the Progressives. Most were people of modest means, not entrepreneurs or professionals. They were not the downtown boosters of development and growth; they were the people who organized to block the freeway from going through town, to oppose the redevelopment project that would tear down cheap houses, and to fight the condos and public housing projects that would bring unwelcome neighbors. They did not believe in expert government delivering social engineering solutions to California's problems; they were the people who picketed and marched against busing students to desegregate schools. "It was this *fusion* of grievances in an unstable economic climate, and not just the tax crisis alone," historian Mike Davis wrote, "that explains the extraordinarily high emotional temperature in the Southern California suburbs during the summer of 1978."[9]

Acting alone, they had often lost their battles to big business and the well-heeled developers with connections at city hall. But rising property taxes brought them together. Cutting those taxes was not just about protecting their homes. It was also a way to cut off the flow of dollars that funded school busing and fueled sprawl and development in their neighborhoods. And the surge of property taxes brought new allies to their side—wealthy suburbanites finally feeling the tax pinch, real estate brokers, Howard Jarvis's apartment house owners—allies with the skills and resources to help them finally prevail.

They owed but one thing to the Progressives. If Governor Jerry Brown, who took office in 1975, and the legislature would not listen or could not act, they could take their case to the ballot, just as Hiram Johnson had intended.

FAILURE OF LEADERSHIP

This time around, unlike in 1968 and 1972, Sacramento was slow to hear the rising homeowner rage. "I think a lot of us in Sacramento . . . really didn't measure the distress of homeowners accurately enough," former Assembly speaker Leo McCarthy would later remember. "[We] sort of said, 'Well, they've got this big asset, a home, that's being greatly inflated now, and that's going to be good for their kids, their families, whoever inherits it,' and so on. We didn't understand, and should have, the fears of a lot of these homeowners."[10]

Jerry Brown was equally tone deaf. Gunther Buerk, a Rancho Palos Verdes civic leader, recalled: "I, at one time, was invited to a party where Governor Brown was there and we had a three-quarters of an hour debate, he and I, and everybody gathered around, on this issue. . . . He could not understand—that somebody, let's say, who makes $40,000, $50,000 a year, lives in an area like this, and suddenly gets hit with a $6,000 tax bill—that something has to give."[11] It was not until lawmakers campaigned in 1976 that "they realized things were in a desperate state and that they were being blamed for them," said Peter Behr, a Republican state senator from Marin County.[12] Finally understanding the plight of homeowners was a step toward a solution. But delivering enough money to relieve their burden required a giant leap.

At least lawmakers had the wind at their backs. The boom and inflation that were driving up home prices and property taxes were also filling the state government's coffers. California's progressive income tax had no inflation indexing. As a result, as workers got raises, many of them also got bumped into a higher income tax bracket and paid a higher share of their income to the state. Inflation was providing state government with an annual tax increase, which no lawmaker had to vote for. In January 1977 the Brown administration officially estimated that the state had a surplus of $940 million, equivalent to almost one-tenth of the annual budget. In truth, the surplus was much bigger and growing every day. It would reach $7.1 billion, or half a year's budget, by the time Prop 13 passed.

But two things stood in the way of action. One was a governor more interested in big ideas and the grand sweep of technology and history than in the boring details of tax policy or the grunt work of passing legislation. Brown didn't want to squander the whole surplus on helping homeowners. "The single biggest difficulty we had was the Department of Finance said you can't commit more than $300 or $400 million to property tax relief," remembered State Treasurer Bill Lockyer, then a member of the Assembly. "It was such a small amount that you really couldn't provide significant enough relief for people to really think it mattered."[13] Brown had his own priorities—cutting the tax on business inventories and shooting California's very own communications satellite into space. A large surplus, at a time when New York City was broke, could be held up in his impending reelection campaign as evidence of his tightfistedness. (Brown now maintains that he was holding on to the surplus because he anticipated an economic downturn.)[14] The tax-relief bill the administration introduced in January 1977 proposed to devote most of its assistance to households that paid the highest property taxes in relation to their incomes. Most homeowners would get only about two hundred dollars.

Lawmakers overwhelmingly favored reducing homeowners' swollen property tax bills. But the money had to come from somewhere; for homeowners to win, someone else had to lose. Liberals proposed to target homeowner tax relief on lower-income households and pay for it by raising income taxes on the wealthy and corporations, and by limiting how much money local governments could raise. Conservatives wanted more of the property tax relief to go to middle- and high-income homeowners, and they wanted even stricter limits on government spending. Local governments wanted to protect their revenue.

After a whole legislative session of fighting back and forth, a first compromise bill came out of conference committee in September 1977 but failed to win a majority in the Senate. A second try at a compromise satisfied the Assembly, where Speaker McCarthy had the needed votes for passage and the governor's commitment to sign the bill.

But the bill ran aground in the Senate, hung up on the second obstacle: California's requirement for a two-thirds majority to pass any spending bill. (Using state money to give taxpayers relief from the local property tax counted as spending under legislative rules.) Republicans objected to targeting relief to the households that needed it most, and to providing assistance to renters. At a low ebb politically, they also knew that voters would likely blame the majority Democrats if the legislature failed to deliver a solution. All of them voted against the compromise.

"Had this been an ordinary statute requiring a simple majority in each house," McCarthy later said. "I believe we could have done a great deal to remedy the plight of many homeowners in the state over the opposition of business property taxpayers." Because of California's undemocratic rules, homeowners would suffer another year of soaring property taxes, despite having a majority of their elected representatives on their side.[15]

Democratic lawmakers urged Brown to call out the Republicans for their obstruction and summon legislators to a special session to provide tax relief. He didn't. The legislature would not return until January 1978, after Jarvis and Gann had qualified their initiative for the June ballot. After a few weeks of haggling, lawmakers finally agreed on a tax-relief bill. It cut homeowners' property tax rates by 30 percent, raised the homeowner exemption, created a renter's tax credit, and provided for a complex split-roll property tax, in which residential and nonresidential business property could be taxed at different rates and limits would be placed on revenues. The legislative alternative would become law only if voters in the June election approved Proposition 8, a constitutional amendment authorizing the split roll, and defeated Prop 13.

"But at this stage it was too little, too late," Peter Behr, author of the alternative, said later. "The governor was very weak. After [it] passed . . . he came out of his office, surrounded by reporters, it was the greatest thing since sliced bread, and he was going to campaign vigorously for it. And the governor meant it. No one could doubt his sincerity, but he didn't do a damn thing." Prop 8 offered homeowners only half as much property tax reduction as Prop 13. Because of an unfocused governor and the two-thirds rule, desperate homeowners were left with little choice. Against the advice of Jerry Brown and Pete Wilson (then mayor of San Diego and a candidate for governor) and George Deukmejian (then a state senator and candidate for attorney general), and ignoring the warnings from business, labor, and the California Taxpayers' Association that the Jarvis-Gann measure would lead to fiscal chaos and endanger public safety, Californians rolled the Prop 13 dice.[16]

THE CATASTROPHE THAT WASN'T

The voters who thronged to the polls to vote for Prop 13 weren't looking to remake California. Only a small minority of them shared Jarvis and Gann's desire to slash the size of government; most actually favored more public services (and believed they could magically have something for nothing). They were simply set on lowering the out-of-control property taxes on their homes, something they had long been asking their elected leaders to do. When their elected leaders failed, Prop 13 was the only game in town. On June 6, 1978, they passed it by an almost two-to-one margin.[17]

The most immediate effect of Prop 13 was the one voters had most fervently sought. It slashed property taxes, from an average of about 2.6 percent of market value to the new legislated rate of 1 percent of the property's 1975 value, plus the mill rate needed to retire any outstanding local general obligation bonds. In the first five years after Prop 13 passed, the average homeowner saved about $10,000, almost enough at the time to buy two subcompact cars. The biggest winner, however, was business. Businesses had already seen their share of assessments fall after AB 80 took effect, and they had not experienced the same inflation-driven runup experienced by homeowners. Nevertheless, they received 63 percent of the tax savings from Prop 13, about twice as much as homeowners.[18]

The big losers were local governments. With a single vote, they had lost revenue amounting to 22 percent of their budgeted expenditures. "The local governments were shell-shocked," Leo McCarthy remembered. "And of course, they all came to Sacramento looking for help."[19]

Some leaders would have been content to let local governments go it alone, although for very different reasons. Howard Jarvis reveled in the cuts to services and schools. He applauded the axing of school electives ("frills") and the elimination of summer school ("nothing more than a baby-sitting program"). On the other side of the political spectrum, some liberals wanted voters to understand what they had done. "I was part of the minority view, which was . . . don't bail out local agencies," Bill Lockyer said. "People should see consequences of their votes."[20]

The majority of lawmakers in Sacramento felt otherwise. With a huge surplus piling up in state coffers, and interest groups pounding on the doors of the state capitol, there was never any doubt that the state would step in to soften the blow. Sacramento assumed the lead role in funding the schools and relieved counties of some of the costs of health and welfare programs. The catastrophe that Prop 13's opponents had warned of never happened.[21]

Even if catastrophe was adverted, California was changed, in ways big and small. Schools axed their sixth period, in which students had taken electives like music and art; eliminated summer school programs that had allowed students to take advanced courses like physics and chemistry; laid off counselors, nurses, and librarians; and reduced maintenance and book purchases. Community colleges ended adult education classes and fired counselors. Police departments cut back on chasing burglars and drug pushers. Cities reduced street cleaning and repaving, and deferred repairs on public buildings. Parks went unmowed and unwatered, and gymnasiums were shuttered. Los Angeles, for example, reduced its park staff by half and shut down many of the recreation programs that formerly kept kids busy and under adult supervision when they weren't at school. By 1987 the city had seventy-five "dead parks," littered places where drugs were sold and gangs had assumed the role of organizing youth activities.[22]

Things that Californians born after 1970 now simply take for granted— that you have to pay to get a police report or a permit to carry a weapon; pay when the paramedics whisk you to the hospital after you fall off your bike and break an arm; pay to swim at the public pool, hold a meeting at a community center, play on the softball diamond, or take an exercise class; pay at school for a towel to shower after gym or for an apron in chemistry lab or for a field trip—all started with Prop 13. It's when the police department stopped sending out an officer after your home got broken into and cities started closing the library nights and several days a week.

The loss of public goods mattered less to people with good incomes. In wealthier communities, people raised private money or passed tax override measures, as Prop 13 permitted, to keep up their neighborhood parks or reopen the library at night. The move toward public squalor mattered much more to people with lower incomes, most of whom got no tax cut. For them, California became a meaner, shabbier, more dangerous place, one with fewer opportunities to get ahead. A tax revolt set off by low- and middle-income homeowners had become, in the hands of Jarvis and Gann, a lever to widen the gap between the haves and the have-nots.[23]

WRITING A NEW OPERATING SYSTEM

The initial budget decisions made in the wake of Prop 13 have been reshaped over the years, as elected officials and voters approved laws and initiative measures to shave off some of the sharp edges. What remain, however, are the far-reaching changes Prop 13 made in the way California governs—or now too often fails to govern—itself. When California voters went to the polls in June 1978 to cut their property taxes, little did most of them know that they were also writing a new operating system for California government.

Oddly, Prop 13's limit on property taxes was not its central feature. At the core of the new system was the requirement for a two-thirds vote in each legislative chamber to raise revenue. It made California the only state to require a two-thirds vote for both spending and tax bills. This supermajority rule was layered on top of California's existing system, in the same way that Microsoft's Windows operating system was initially layered on top of the DOS systems used in early PCs. By providing the familiar point-and-click graphical user interface, Windows aimed at making computing easier. The Prop 13 system, however, would make it harder for the legislature to make decisions.

California's legislature had labored under a two-thirds supermajority requirement for budget and spending legislation since the 1930s—the same one that prevented the legislature in 1977 from taking swift action to help homeowners. The initial version was a spending limit. Placed in the constitution in 1933 as part of a larger scheme known as the Riley-Stewart plan, it capped increases in nonschool spending at 5 percent from one two-year budget to the next, unless the appropriation was approved by two-thirds of legislators. In practice, however, the two-thirds hurdle was not a high one. Budgets routinely grew by more than 5 percent, something both parties recognized as necessary to keep up with California's spectacular growth. When the 1960s constitution revision commission amended out the 5 percent limit, extending the supermajority requirement to all non-school appropriations, the change did not even merit mention in the 1966 ballot pamphlet voters had before them as they approved the revision.

Prop 13, and the nationwide tax revolt that followed, shattered that consensus. Its passage provided a boost to the GOP in California, which elected a host of new legislators in 1978 known as the "Prop 13 babies." (Their opponents also called them "the Cavemen," a title they soon proudly brandished.) Republicans, including the former California governor who would be elected president in 1980, adopted a strong anti-tax message. Democrats responded by trying to protect generous levels of services and benefits (with the notable exception of Jerry Brown, who declared himself a "born-again tax cutter" and spent much of 1979 outside Sacramento, squiring rock star Linda Ronstadt to Africa and preparing his own run for president in 1980). Prop 13 had made taxes a partisan issue. But it also had, in establishing a two-thirds vote requirement, required greater consensus from the legislature. At once politically polarizing and legally consensus-requiring, Prop 13 was at war with itself.

Soon, so was the legislature. As time went on, the minority party used the two-thirds rule to paralyze the legislature.

The minority party—the Republicans in all years but two—learned slowly. In 1980, Senate Republicans refused to support the budget because of several spending items, dropping their holdout only when spending any more time in Sacramento would have meant missing the Republican National Convention.[24] But the minority party became more aggressive in the 1990s, when a recession, combined with the post-Cold War shrinking of the defense and aerospace industries in the state, led to a decline in state revenues.

In most budget fights, the Republicans—holding more than one-third of the seats in one or both legislative chambers, so enough to block a budget or revenue increase—would make their support contingent on a list of demands. Many involved either cutting taxes or boosting spending for their own constituents—even in times when the budget was out of balance. Sometimes, Republicans demanded cuts in programs prized by Democrats. This form of hostage-taking became the norm. As long as the minority party could remain cohesive, the strategy would work. The legislative majority felt the burden of governing the state. But the minority could delay the most basic task of the legislature—passing a budget—without being held responsible.

Twice, in 1992 and again in 2009, the Republicans held out so long that the state would run short on cash and be forced to pay government bills with IOUs. Democrats could do little but complain. "It is wholly unreasonable for the largest state in the union, with the eighth-largest economy in the world, to give the party that the voters have decided is the minority party the ability to dictate not only when the budget will be passed, but what will be in it," said Senate President Pro Tem Darrell Steinberg in 2009. "It's an extraordinary concept, when you think about it."[25]

Republicans would counter that they were protecting the state from high taxes and higher spending—even though their demands to close budgets often led to higher spending, particularly in the inland districts Republicans represented. The budget compromises eventually adopted each year often had hidden costs, through questionable borrowing and accounting gimmicks, such as changing state workers' pay period by one day so only eleven checks had to be counted in a fiscal year. These gimmicks, whose effects ran into the billions of dollars, were called "budget solutions" but were, in fact, evidence that the real solutions could not command supermajority support.

This two-thirds system, as it hardened, obscured responsibility and prevented political accountability. In a majority-vote system, the Democrats would have been accountable for the state's budget problems. If the budget went south or taxes got too high, Republicans could legitimately blame Democrats and make a clean case for voters to hand them the reins of the legislature, as they did when they took over the U.S. House of Representatives in 1994.

But in a two-thirds system, no one could fairly say that a budget belonged to one party or the other. Both parties had their names on the birth certificate. And so Republicans couldn't gain politically by rallying against the budget status quo. Instead, they clung to the two-thirds system for the leverage it provided. In this way, the minority party had a "Stockholm syndrome" relationship with the supermajority require-ment; they loved what kept them in political prison.

The two-thirds formula, by demanding consensus, protected both parties from full accountability for fiscal decisions. It was a license for irresponsibility and inaction. Ken Maddy, GOP Senate leader during the tough budget years of the early nineties, later complained of the difficulty of rounding up the Republican votes needed to pass the compromises worked out by Governor Pete Wilson and legislative leaders. "There are some of my colleagues, particularly those on the far right, who never did have a bill that they cared about or wanted to pass," he said. "All they were concerned about was stopping bills. They were 'no' votes. Well, if you're only concerned about 'no' votes, then I had no leverage."[26]

When nothing happened, neither side could be blamed. And when nothing happened, initiative sponsors had all the reason they needed to circumvent the legislature and take their proposal directly to the people.

The timing couldn't have been worse. The two-thirds requirement for revenue increases undermined the legislature's ability to decide big issues—precisely at the time that Prop 13, as an example of a success-ful political and media enterprise, turned the initiative process into an alternative to the legislature. Prop 13's success, not unlike the discovery of gold, created a rush of interest from the state's movers and shakers—politicians, advocates, donors, pollsters, media consultants, reporters. The legislature and the initiative became competitors; the contest was over which would have primacy of place as the center of political debate and discussion.

EMPOWERING SACRAMENTO

The big idea behind this shift toward supermajority rules and restric-tions was that a simple majority of legislators couldn't be trusted to set California's course. But here's the irony: the same measure that signaled voter mistrust of the legislature also gave state government even broader control over California life. By slashing local property tax revenues, putting up higher barriers for local passage of taxes and bonds, and giving the legislature the authority to divvy up remaining property tax dollars, Prop 13 was the Great Centralizer.

This transfer of power from the county building and the school district office to the state capitol could not have come as a surprise to anyone. Prop 13 plainly announced that the property tax rate, formerly set by local governments, was now to be locked into the constitution, and that property tax revenues were henceforth to be "apportioned according to law to the districts within the counties"—the legislature being the state's lawgiver. The ballot pamphlet noted the probability that Prop 13's revenue cuts would force the state to fill the void. During the Prop 13 campaign, opponents warned voters that they were handing over more of the reins of government to the very state politicians whose inaction fueled their anger. "What would happen to local control of local government under Proposition 13?" the California Taxpayers' Association, a probusiness group, asked during the campaign. "Is there any way to prevent greater state control?"[27] But voters did not have the nuances of government structure on their minds; they were focused on reducing their property tax.

The shift started within days of Prop 13's triumph. The legislature quickly enacted a temporary bailout bill for local government, with strings attached. "We specified that no firemen or policemen could be fired throughout the state. That was sacrosanct," Peter Behr remembered.[28] The 1978 bailout also put limits on school district spending (with bigger cuts in wealthy districts than in poor ones), barred local governments from giving workers a raise above the rate of inflation, and required them to use their reserves to soften program cuts.

"Policy usually follows money, and when the state government became responsible for paying a much larger portion of school district budgets and county budgets, that meant increased state control over those two levels of government," said Leo McCarthy.[29] Enraged by these handcuffs on local control, several cities in Southern California turned down the money, choosing instead to give raises and cut programs. (The state supreme court soon struck down the restrictions on pay increases.)

A permanent bailout bill followed a year later. Using the new power given to it by Prop 13, the legislature divvied up the remaining property tax, giving most of it to counties and cities according to their prior spending levels. The state took over the primary duty for funding schools, which were now left with little local tax revenue of their own, and it relieved counties of paying a share of some health and welfare programs. Where once there had been largely separate and relatively well defined pots of revenue—one labeled "local," the other "state"—there was now a single hydraulic money system, as vast as the state's waterworks, with the legislature controlling the sluices and valves. "I don't think local government has ever been restored to independence," Peter Behr said.[30]

In many ways, this centralization of power in Sacramento represented a liberal dream come true. For years liberals had been fighting to have the state take a greater role in funding and regulating schools and health and welfare programs, to equalize funding between wealthy and poor school districts and to force stingy counties to provide adequate services to the poor, sick, aged, and disabled. Jarvis and Gann gave them what they wanted. Through the bailout the state took the biggest step yet toward complying with the California supreme court's 1971 and 1976 *Serrano* decisions, which had held that the disparities in per pupil school funding produced by relying on the property tax were unconstitutional. Yet because of the reduction in revenues, equalization ended up being more about leveling down than raising up.[31]

What liberals had long sought, conservatives had feared. But conservatives came to accept big government in Sacramento because they hated taxes more. Having once opposed Prop 13, business groups such as the California Taxpayers' Association embraced it. They decried several state supreme court decisions that opened small windows in Prop 13 for cities to enact local taxes. Cornell Mayer, chairman of the board of Kaiser Aluminum and then leader of the Business Roundtable, representing the state's largest corporations, said, "I think the bulk of our taxes should be raised on a statewide level." With power centralized in the legislature, where any revenue increase required a supermajority vote, business no longer had to worry so much about what mischief local leaders might be up to. Sacramento offered one-stop influence shopping—and equally important, one-stop blocking of actions they opposed.[32]

Even if conservatives and business had a philosophical quarrel with concentrating power at the state capitol, the new Prop 13 operating system made leaning on Sacramento essential for the things they needed from government, including public safety, water, and transportation.

Take the example of infrastructure. Because of Prop 13, local governments could no longer sell general obligation bonds, repaid through the property tax, to build the public infrastructure—everything from roads to firehouses—needed to sustain growth. To the dismay of builders, local officials turned, as an alternative, to devices like impact fees on developers to pay for those things. That brought the developers, builders, and their political allies scurrying to Sacramento for infrastructure solutions that didn't land on their shoulders, such as restoring to school and community college districts the power to issue general obligation bonds to build and remodel schools. For three decades the state capitol has been the battlefield where business interests have fought—over developer fees and local school bond authority and local transportation sales taxes and state infrastructure investment—in an effort to have their tax cuts and their public works too. Voters have not been alone in wanting something for nothing.

Centralizing power has been very good for one lucky business group: the owners of real estate near the state capitol. Sacramento's once sleepy downtown, where private office development was mostly moribund for a half-century, sprouted new high-rise office buildings to bivouac the lobbyist-warriors that special interests have hired, since Prop 13, to joust on the expanded battlefield.

As of October 2009 there were 1,049 lobbyists registered with the secretary of state, about nine for each member of the legislature. Their clients spent a total of $553 million during the 2007–08 legislative session to influence state policy, more than taxpayers spent to support the legislature itself. (In 1977–78 there were 195 lobbyists whose clients spent $49.6

million to influence the legislature.) About one dollar in ten of lobbying spending is by cities, counties, and school districts begging the capitol for money and policies that local leaders, before Prop 13, once directly controlled. These figures do not count the generals at the strategic consulting firms, who map the plan of lobbying battle but do not have to sully themselves by registering as lobbyists; the public relations experts who soften up the targets with psychological warfare tactics of disinformation, spin, and the creation of phantom regiments of supporters; the fund-raisers and party planners who manage the finances and logistics of sustaining the conflict; the reporters and pundits who show up after the battles to count the dead and shoot the wounded.[33]

Centralization has not been as good for other Californians. Prop 13 and the resulting concentration of power in the state capitol made government opaque, inflexible, and unaccountable.

"California is too big and too complex for Sacramento to be exercising, through policy, power over school districts," Leo McCarthy said, naming just one of the areas of California life in which state government now takes the lead role.[34] And as difficult as it is for state policy makers to understand the problems and needs of thousands of schools from Alturas to South Central Los Angeles, it is now even harder for citizens to make sense of how government works. If students at your neighborhood school are not learning as much as you think they should, who's responsible? And how can you make that situation change? Those questions are nearly impossible for the average Californian to answer. California's new operating system, delivered in a spasm of voter frustration, has proved best at breeding more frustration.

EMPOWERING PUBLIC EMPLOYEES

Among all the ironies of Prop 13, however, one is particularly delicious. By separating the responsibility for taxing and spending at the local level and by centralizing power at the state capitol, Prop 13 opened the way for public employees—teachers, police, firefighters, prison guards, city managers—to increase their influence, both in local government and in Sacramento. They have used that power to raise their compensation to levels unequaled in the rest of the country. Next to the shrunken property tax bill on Prop 13's trophy shelf sits a gold-plated public pension.

Although they had been among Prop 13's fiercest opponents, public employee unions, like business groups, have made good use of the centralization of power in Sacramento. Business and taxpayer groups came to like the concentration of authority at the state level as a way to stop local governments from raising their taxes. Public unions found it a convenient way to win at the capitol what was formerly hard to win at the bargaining table, local employer by local employer, negotiation by negotiation.

For example, in 1982 California became the first state to enact a law requiring local governments to treat any cancer in firefighters as a disability caused by their jobs. Since then, unions have succeeded in extending presumptive disability to other public safety workers and other diseases. When a chain-smoking, hard-drinking, french-fry scarfing, bed-hopping cop comes down with lung cancer, clogged coronary arteries, and hepatitis, taxpayers are on the hook for all the costs. (Under the terms of Paul Gann's 1979 Proposition 4, a spending limit that he called "The Spirit of 13" measure, these are state mandates, which the state is required to pay out of its own revenues.)

The effects of Prop 13 have been felt most strongly, though, in local politics. Before the Jarvis-Gann measure, local agencies and their boards had dual duties. They decided how much to spend on public services, and they set the property tax rate needed to supply that money. And because they had the power to tax, they attracted a lot of attention, not just from people interested in the quality of the services, but also from property owners, both business and homeowners, who paid the taxes to support those services. In the two decades before Prop 13, tens of thousands of them showed up at public meetings to protest their tax bills. "I remember that there really were leading businesspeople in the community, leading professional people, who served on the school board because of this taxing authority," said Gary Hart, who served in both the Assembly and state Senate.[35]

Prop 13 and successor measures (Proposition 62 in 1986 and Proposition 218 in 1996) took away taxing authority from local elected officials, leaving them with the reduced responsibility of spending dollars whose amount was set in Sacramento or by the voters. (School boards had begun to lose their taxing authority with the *Serrano* equalization decision in 1971.) Without the power to tax, local governments were less of an immediate threat to local pocketbooks. It was no longer necessary for business and taxpayer groups to watch them so carefully.

And so leaders of business groups began a retreat from local service. "Beginning in the early to mid-seventies and culminating with Proposition 13," Hart said, "leaders in the community, people in the Rotary [clubs], said, 'This is not a good use of my time; this is no fun. All we're doing is cutting.' Who needs that?" School board members in California are now less likely to be business people or professionals than they are in the country as a whole.[36]

The retreat of what might be called the "taxpayer interest" left the field in local politics to those whose primary interest in local government is as a source of income or subsidy—including developers, contractors, and especially, public employees. They provided the biggest contributions to local candidates and delivered the most bodies to staff phone banks and walk precincts. Often the candidates and elected officials were public employees themselves. In suburban Sacramento, for example, it became common for firefighters from one jurisdiction to run for and win seats on the boards of other jurisdictions providing fire protection, where they handed out big raises that then become the standard for wages in their own department. In 2008, Sacramento Metropolitan Fire District paid firefighters a median wage of $114,169 and fire-truck drivers a median of $144,274; the average annual wage in the county was about $52,000. Operating with little scrutiny from their own residents or from the atrophying commercial news media, local governments dominated by their employees made pay and pension commitments that they could not keep.

Vallejo was forced to declare bankruptcy in 2008, and San Diego, the state's second-biggest city, dubbed "Enron by the Sea," teetered on the precipice.[37]

The growing power of local employees to snatch scarce tax dollars for their own benefit has hurt the ability of governments to deliver needed services to their residents. But it has also reinforced the trend toward centralization of authority in Sacramento. In May 1997, when a surging economy brought in an extra $2 billion that Governor Pete Wilson, under Proposition 98, was required to spend on schools, he insisted on using the bonanza in ways dictated by Sacramento, most of it to reduce class sizes in primary grades. It was an odd choice. Wilson and his education experts had spent years saying that school districts needed relief from overbearing regulation by Sacramento. But in this instance he did exactly the opposite. Certain that local school boards couldn't be trusted to resist their teacher unions, Wilson wanted to keep the dollars off the bargaining table. He was not alone. As the revenue surge of the Internet boom years continued, the next Democratic administration also tried to ensure that a large share of new school dollars would be used as Sacramento directed and not given to districts as general aid. "School superintendents would often say publicly, 'This is outrageous,'" said Gary Hart, who also served as Governor Gray Davis's first education secretary. "And then they would call up and say, 'Please, don't put all this new money on the collective bargaining table.'"[38]

The class-size reduction turned into one of the most expensive boondoggles in recent history. To keep the money off the bargaining table, the program had to be implemented overnight. But with unemployment low, California didn't have tens of thousands of qualified teachers on the shelf to pour into the new jobs it was creating. Schools were forced to hire untrained teachers on emergency credentials. As credentialed teachers with seniority flocked to newly opened jobs in high-income neighborhoods, the unprepared teachers landed disproportionately in the poorest schools, to teach students who most needed experienced instructors. (Despite Governor Wilson's efforts to keep money away from them, the teachers' unions won anyway, their numbers and dues collections swollen by all the new members.)

Yes, the crooked assessors were out and property taxes were down. But taking taxing authority away from local government handed over local power to public employees; which led the state to take more policy authority; which made local government a less attractive place for anyone but public employees to serve; and which bred top-down policies that wasted tax dollars. In the jargon of computer programmers, the new Prop 13 operating system was an endless loop, leading to a crash.

4

FROM TEACHERS TO JANITORS

Direct Democracy Demotes the Legislature

William "Sandy" Muir, a political scientist at the University of California, Berkeley, has an unusual method of academic study. When he wants to write a book on an institution, he takes a job inside it. So in 1975, Muir, eager to do a book on how state legislatures work, wrangled a job as a consultant to the California State Assembly's powerful committee on finance, insurance, and commerce.

The experience was eye-opening. A rare Republican in the academic world, Muir had worked previously for Ronald Reagan's successful 1966 campaign for governor and for the Oakland police department. Muir understood better than most the rising anti-tax and anti-government populism on the right. He also knew that complaining about elected legislators had been a favorite American pastime for the entire history of the country. But Muir could not help but be impressed by day-to-day life in the California legislature.

What struck him first were the professionalism and long experience of his co-workers. The California legislature was hardly a group of yahoo pols, as the more cynical members of the public imagined them. They were serious people working for a serious institution. The 1960s constitutional revision had made the legislature a full-time body, and its speakers, especially Jesse Unruh and Leo McCarthy, had beefed up its committee system into a real force for careful legislation. New lawmakers spent a decade or more apprenticing in the committees before they developed enough expertise to take leadership positions. The staffers they hired were often experts in their fields. And all legislation was submitted to lawyers and analysts who conducted rigorous, nonpartisan analysis. During Muir's two years, the legislature produced groundbreaking legislation on agricultural labor relations, prisons, unemployment insurance, tort reform, euthanasia, oil taxes, and decriminalization of marijuana.

"The California legislature comes closest to having all the characteristics a legislature should have," concluded the Citizens Conference on State Government in a study Muir quoted approvingly. "It is . . . both a 'citizen' and a 'professional' legislature; it makes informed decisions, and it makes them democratically; it listens to its public, and it leads it."[1]

Taken as a whole, the California legislature reminded Muir of nothing so much as a university, a place where lawmakers and staffers educated each other and, by extension, the public. The instruction worked in three ways. First, the introduction and review of thousands of bills allowed for education on a wide array of issues. Second, by giving each legislator responsibility for carrying a certain number of bills, the legislative process taught lawmakers the methods and tactics of public negotiation. Third, by dividing the review of bills into committees, the legislature, over time, turned its members into true experts.

In 1982 Muir published a study in which he called California's legislature "the nation's best"; it was more responsive to the public, offered more expertise, and was more effective than any other body, he argued. He titled his book, which would become a primer for understanding the body: *Legislature: California's School for Politics.* "The California Legislature is the finest in the world," Muir would later say. "It works."[2]

Even before his book appeared, Muir's cherished professional legislature was under attack, though he didn't fully realize it at the time. Good-government groups saw the campaign money that funded legislative campaigns and empowered its leaders as corrupt. Supporters of education and health care and transportation had grown frustrated at the body—and then at Governor Jerry Brown—for building an "obscene surplus," as it was known, instead of pouring more money into their programs. And the legislature, for all its professionalism, seemed small for a state population that had surpassed 20 million, on its way to more than 38 million. The combination of California's relentless population growth and its legislature of 120 members—the same size it had been when the 1879 constitution was written and the state's population had been less than 1 million—had produced the nation's most populous legislative districts.

Still, the legislature in the early 1980s seemed to be, if anything, more powerful and important than ever before. As we have seen with its post–Prop 13 bailout of local governments, the legislature had more decisions to make over funding and policy than ever before. And state supreme court decisions had, in the name of equalizing education in poor and rich districts, transferred authority over education from local school boards to Sacramento.

But making so many big decisions would prove more and more difficult with the passage of time. Muir, who had worked in the state capitol in 1975 and 1976 but did not publish his book until 1982, wrote with concern that by 1980 his beloved legislature "seemed shaky and fragile.... The massive job of reconstructing the fiscal relationships between state and local governments, made necessary by a radical tax reform [Prop 13], defied quick accomplishment."[3]

Part of the problem was that Prop 13 had established a two-thirds supermajority to pass tax increases, which made it harder to reach consensus on how to fund the needs of that growing population. Even more profoundly, Prop 13 had touched off a surge of ballot initiatives by interests and activists who suddenly saw the opportunity to reshape California government with one measure, whether the legislature went along or not. Before too long, this initiative surge began to weaken the most important institution in a representative democracy, the legislature. Lawmakers slowly lost their control over pieces of the law, then over the budget. Eventually initiative sponsors would take dead aim at legislative know-how, seeking to shut down Muir's "school for politics" with a term-limits measure.

The professor had considered eight possible threats to the legislature in his book. But, Muir would explain later, he had not included a ninth—term limits—because the notion of diminishing legislative experience and expertise in such a way seemed tantamount to destroying the legislature as an institution. And that, Muir would say, "seemed unthinkable."[4]

THE INITIATIVE
AS ENTREPRENEURIAL TOOL

In 1983, Fred Kimball and his sons were discussing how to drum up business for their signature-gathering firm, Kimball Petition Management. Theirs was just one of dozens of enterprises that had sprung up in California to serve a new generation of political entrepreneurs who wanted to make their own Prop 13s. There were firms, like Kimball, devoted to gathering signatures outside of shopping malls and grocery stores to qualify initiatives for the ballot. Direct mail companies sent out initiatives to raise money, sign up supporters, and build new political organizations that could, in turn, raise more money and sign up more supporters for more initiatives. Law firms specializing in election law devoted themselves to the drafting and vetting of new measures. Media consultants made advertisements and purchased TV time. Political pros who previously labored in candidate campaigns began to specialize instead in initiatives. It was easier work. For one thing, there were no limits on the size of contributions, so a campaign could be supported with a handful of big gifts, removing the pressures of constant fund-raising. For another, ballot initiatives made better clients than flesh-and-blood politicians. The consultants were fond of joking that initiatives didn't have their own ideas, emotions, or meddling wives (or husbands).

The new initiative industry was a volume business. Although the number of initiatives was surging in the years after Prop 13, the Kimballs could always use more clients. Fred Kimball was determined not to wait for activists or experts with ideas to come to him. He wanted to dream up his own initiatives and then sell the idea to interests or companies that had the deep pockets to pay his company to qualify them.

"We were sitting around one day, bored, trying to think about what we were going to do next," Kimball's son, Kelly, once told the *San Francisco Chronicle*, when one idea occurred: an initiative to establish a state lottery.[5] Other states had lotteries, but in California the horseracing industry and Nevada gaming interests had fought off legislative proposals to create one. The Kimballs ordered up polling that showed a state lottery would be popular if its profits went to education. So they filed the lottery initiative with the state attorney general, paying the $200 filing fee, and went looking for a client to pay them to put it before the voters. The natural client was Scientific Games, a Georgia company that supplies the printed materials and technologies to put on lotteries. After brief negotiations, Scientific Games decided to fund the Kimballs' state lottery initiative, giving more than $2 million for signature gathering and a campaign. In November 1984, Californians voted themselves a lottery.

It was the perfect transaction for the post–Prop 13 age of California politics. The Kimballs got business for their firm. Scientific Games got the most populous state in the Union as a customer. To this day, the company is the lottery's top printer. "No. 1, of course, it was business," said Fred's son, also named Fred Kimball, who still runs Kimball Petition Management. "But we also got the lottery on the ballot and helped education at the same time."[6]

Putting business before policy is not a problem exclusive to the initiative process. Policy outcomes are purchased in the California legislature and in other deliberative bodies all over the world. What is different about initiative measures such as the lottery is that, in California, they are so profoundly hard to undo. By approving a lottery initiative, voters did far more than establish a lottery or approve a new funding source for education. They effectively—and forever—stripped state lawmakers of the power to make policy choices about how to manage the lottery, use the funds it generates, and adjust to changes in the market like the rise of tribal gaming casinos and online gambling.

California's singular initiative process was responsible for this inflexibility. Yes, some twenty-six other states permit the initiative, the referendum, or both. And in many states, such powers have been used to tie the hands of legislators and to make irresponsible budget allocations, as in California. But California's initiative process was unique for the way it was set apart from the normal give-and-take of government and politics.

Any statute approved by initiative—even a major statute as consequential as the creation of a new form of state-sponsored gambling—cannot be amended or altered by the legislature without another vote of the people.[7] That isn't true in any other state. So a California initiative doesn't merely circumvent state lawmakers at a particular time and place. It creates a new, higher class of law, exempt from independent amendment or fix by the legislature, no matter how problematic or outdated it becomes.

The lottery initiative was doubly bad; not only did it establish the lottery, but it also set up a host of rules for how the lottery games would be run, what sort of technology could be used, and how lottery money would be spent. None of these rules could be changed by the legislature, even when they created problems for the lottery. When other states adopted Internet and other technological changes, California lawmakers couldn't respond to the competition. When rules on payouts limited the lottery's profits and thus its contributions to education, lawmakers pointed out the problem but couldn't act by themselves.

If anything, the lottery, as enacted by initiative, may have hurt education more than it helps. The lottery generates a little more than $1 billion annually for K–12 education—less than 2 percent of annual education spending in California. No one knows how the money affects the classroom because school districts are not required to report how they spend it. And because voters mistakenly think the lottery they approved provides big money to education—in polls and focus groups, Californians often guess that the lottery provides 30 percent or more of education funding—the public tends to oppose new, more productive ways of boosting education spending. The lottery initiative may have generated $2 million in business for the Kimballs in 1984, but the legislature and the state must live with its consequences today.

The lottery was only the first of these entrepreneurial initiatives. Political theorists, when considering direct democracy, warn of the tyranny of the majority, but in practice, California's initiative process opened the way for tyranny of the minority, allowing interests to build little empires for themselves. The initiative's power to circumvent the lawmakers, obligate the state for the long term, and create a higher class of law beyond amendment drew many in California to the process. Twenty-four initiatives had qualified for the ballot in the seventies. After Prop 13's success, forty-four initiatives would qualify in the eighties, and sixty-one in the nineties.

Each successful measure tied the hands of the legislature. In some cases, this goal was explicit. In 1979, Prop 13 co-sponsor Paul Gann led a successful campaign to pass Proposition 4 (also known as the Gann initiative), a spending limit on state and local governments. The initiative was complicated—it sought to limit state and local government spending to the 1978–79 levels, with an annual adjustment for population growth and inflation. The larger aim was to shrink government over time. Any revenues that came in above the formula were to be returned to taxpayers. It passed, but the Gann limit didn't bind at first. State spending in the base year had been artificially high because Sacramento had used the "obscene surplus" to bail out local government, and depressed revenues in the early eighties recession left the state well short of what it was permitted to spend. When the economy improved and revenues took off in 1987, state government hit its ceiling. Governor George Deukmejian could have shunted the money that the state couldn't spend to schools and local governments. Instead he sent out tax rebates averaging $71.

The wisdom of such a limit could be debated—but not in the state legislature. The Gann initiative had replaced the judgment of the people's representatives, in the legislature and on local government bodies, with a complicated formula they could not alter or adjust to meet the needs of California as it rapidly changed. The legislature spent its time trying to work within Gann, exploiting its exemption for interest payments on bonds and sending money to local governments that hadn't yet bumped up against their own Gann ceilings. Lawmakers might have debated whether more debt and local government subventions were the best paths to take—if other paths had been open to them.

And when the Gann limit required amendment, lawmakers couldn't do it by themselves. The task had to be left to voters—and the interest groups that had enough money to fund new initiative campaigns. More than anything, the limit fueled more initiatives from interest groups, which sought exemptions from its straitjacket. Spending lobbies, including health advocates and public employee unions, successfully passed two measures—Proposition 99 in 1988 and Proposition 10 in 1998—to exempt new tobacco taxes from the Gann limit. Whatever the policy merits, each new exemption passed by initiative restricted the options of the legislature. It pulled the political center of gravity away from legislative elections and toward the statewide ballot, and it shifted the policy center of gravity away from lawmakers and toward voters.

COMPLEXITY AND
THE SCHOOL FUNDING GUARANTEE

The emblematic initiative of this new age would be Proposition 98, narrowly approved by voters in 1988 with less than 51 percent of the vote. Its author, John Mockler, a longtime state education official and consultant, would describe it as a reaction both to Prop 13's limits on taxation and the Gann limits on spending, and to a weakened legislature produced by these measures and the initiative surge.

Post–Prop 13, the annual budget debate in the legislature usually followed the same script. Lawmakers in the Democratic majority would wait until the very end of the budget process before reaching agreement with the Republican minority on school funding. The Democrats' idea was to make the big, public, political fight over education. The results, however, weren't good for schools. Education funding became a piñata, swinging in the annual budget winds. Schools never knew who would hit it, and how much money would fall out for them. And in bad years, schools often bore the brunt of the public cuts. In the view of Mockler and other leaders in the Sacramento education lobby, politicians loved education so much as an issue that they literally loved it to death.

"Everybody loves education, but everybody fucks education," Mockler would recall years later, in describing the attitude that led to Prop 98. "I say, 'I no longer want to be loved. I'm a hooker. I want to be paid.'"[8]

The California Teachers Association, the largest and most powerful union in the state, hired Mockler to draft a measure. Mockler knew the initiative was a blunt instrument; he would later say that he was not a fan of any initiative, even the ones he'd written. But he also believed that education desperately needed special protection from the budget wars. The initiative Mockler drafted sought to do that by adding a constitutional requirement guaranteeing public schools a share of state revenues. Prop 98 also gave education's funding share a special exemption from the Gann limit. In this way, through the miracle of unintended consequences, restraints spawned new restraints. Before Prop 98, school funding had been the one part of state fiscal policy not subject to a supermajority vote. After Prop 98, school spending, nearly half of the budget, was put on an autopilot that could only be turned off by a two-thirds vote. In effect, Prop 98 left the legislature with very little control over the budget.

Both the Gann limit and Prop 98 were soon modified by another measure, Proposition 111, put on the ballot by the legislature and approved by voters in 1990. That measure relaxed the spending limit, allowing government spending to keep pace with economic and population growth, but made Prop 98 even more complex by grafting a third education funding formula onto Prop 98's two existing formulas. These formulas had nothing to do with the quality of education or school needs.

This new three-headed constitutional education funding guarantee—call it Prop 98 Plus—was so complicated that future lawmakers would be unable to manage it, much less alter it, because most simply couldn't understand it. Mockler himself would say: "Nobody ever really knows what Prop 98 is really." The nonpartisan Legislative Analyst's Office would conclude its official "primer" on Prop 98 with the following surrender: "It involves complex calculations that few fully understand and generates funding results that are often unintuitive or—even worse—counterintuitive." For twenty years California newspapers have reported that Prop 98 guarantees 40 percent of the budget should be spent on education. That is at once not entirely false—there is a provision of Prop 98 that says that—and factually wrong, because that provision of Prop 98 went into effect only twice in the measure's first two decades.

The legislature simply could not govern what it could not understand. Even predicting the budget became impossible. In a state that would come to spend more than $40 billion a year on K–14 education, a 1 percent error in predicting school funding was a $400 million mistake. Mockler made a nice living advising policy makers who didn't understand the formula. "You know, the state is complicated. Life is complicated. The Ten Commandments is complicated," he said. "Because people think Prop 98 is so complicated, I got to send two kids through Stanford."[9]

Prop 98 was the biggest destroyer of legislative discretion, but it was hardly the only one. In 1982, voters limited the legislature's options on taxes by indexing the income tax and eliminating the gift and inheritance taxes. In 1986, voters made the law around tort liability (Proposition 51), taxation for local governments (Proposition 62), and restrictions on toxic discharges (Proposition 65) their own province. In 1988, choosing among five different insurance initiatives, voters enacted a new regime of insurance regulations that could not easily be altered by lawmakers. In 1992, voters would take oversight of much of the state's pension system out of the hands of legislators. In subsequent elections, all manner of topics—medical marijuana, animal protection, juvenile justice, environmental conservation, after-school programs—would be taken off the legislative table by voters. In 1996, annual spending on initiative campaigns in California topped $140 million. For the first time, more was spent on initiatives than was spent by all candidates combined for the 120 seats in the legislature.

With the passage of each measure, a little piece of the legislature died. It wouldn't be long before elected officials themselves, recognizing the writing on the wall, joined in.

THE INITIATIVE AS SELF-PROMOTION

As the legislature's discretion shrank, holding elected office no longer put a politician at the center of the conversation. Earning enough attention to make policy or win a higher office required engaging with the initiative process.

Fame had been part of the appeal of Prop 13. Howard Jarvis himself had been a lifelong publicity seeker, a Utah newspaper publisher who had moved to California. There, he produced a TV show for the Republican Party, ran unsuccessfully for the U.S. Senate in 1962, met actors, and, "star struck," financed an unsuccessful movie called *Ten Little Indians*. But it was Prop 13—and the attendant publicity from its success—that made him a household name and earned him a walk-on, as himself, in the movie *Airplane!*

It was natural that a former movie actor, Ronald Reagan, would be among the first politicians to seek to exploit the power of initiatives. As governor, in 1973 he sponsored Proposition 1, a convoluted budget and taxation measure that voters roundly rejected. He would not be the last to try. In 1990, Attorney General John van de Kamp built his run for governor (he lost the Democratic primary) around his sponsorship of three initiatives. Van de Kamp would later say his only mistake was in sponsoring three measures, which made his message too confusing to voters. "It might have been better if I had done just one," he said.[10]

No politician used the process more than Governor Pete Wilson. Wilson had begun sponsoring ballot campaigns when he was mayor of

San Diego in the 1970s. After eight years in the U.S. Senate, Wilson ran for governor of California in 1990. He made a crime victims' rights initiative a major part of his campaign.[11] In 1992 he sponsored Proposition 165, an initiative to reform welfare and give the governor more powers in the budget process. The Democrats called it a power grab by "King Pete." It lost. In his reelection campaign, he embraced the so-called three-strikes measure to impose longer criminal sentences and Proposition 187, an initiative denying public services to unauthorized immigrants, as integral parts of his campaign. In his second term, he backed initiatives that sought to limit the power of interest groups—particularly public employee unions—that opposed his agenda.

His political adviser George Gorton believed the initiatives were the most important way for Wilson to get attention. Wilson was a tough, blunt, former Marine, but he was a less-than-compelling presence on television. "Voters could remember two, maybe three things about Pete Wilson, and that was it. And so we needed to decide what the two things were and then we needed to hammer those," recalled Gorton. "Initiatives helped us do that."[12]

Rich outsiders found they too could use the process to achieve notoriety—and a desired policy outcome—without the legislature. Silicon Valley produced several multimillionaires who wanted to change education and saw the initiative as the way to do it. Tim Draper, a venture capitalist, sponsored a school voucher initiative amid rumors he might run for office; the measure's defeat ended talk of a candidacy. Ron Unz, a software wizard who lost a run for governor, sponsored a successful 1998 initiative to end bilingual education. Reed Hastings, founder of a software firm and CEO of the Internet-based movie service Netflix, sponsored an initiative to lift the state cap on the total number of charter schools. After he had gathered enough signatures to qualify the measure for the ballot, the legislature—facing the prospect of losing more discretion—caved and passed a bill lifting the cap. Hastings dropped his initiative and helped launch a nonprofit statewide chain of charter schools.

Hollywood would embrace the form. Arnold Schwarzenegger sponsored an initiative to fund after-school programs, Proposition 49, as a way to transition from stardom to the governor's office. The producer Steve Bing would spend more than $50 million of his own money on an unsuccessful 2006 initiative to fund alternative energy programs by taxing oil producers.

The movie director Rob Reiner, famous as "Meathead" from *All in the Family*, sponsored two tobacco tax initiatives, including one to fund new programs in early childhood education. That initiative explicitly prevented the legislature from taking any of the tobacco tax money for other purposes. It also reserved about 20 percent of the tobacco tax money for a statewide commission that Reiner went on to chair. By the time Reiner resigned from the commission in 2006, the body had spent more than $150 million on public relations and advertising campaigns about the importance of health care and early education for young children. By sponsoring a ballot measure, Reiner, a private citizen, gained control over hundreds of millions of tax dollars. Arguably, sponsoring a successful initiative had given him greater direct control over the public purse than any single legislator enjoyed.

THE EPIDEMIC OF "SOMETHING FOR NOTHING"

Although it was a power grab, Reiner's early childhood services initiative was far more responsible than most. The measure included not only the new programs but also the tax revenues to pay for them. This was rare. As the famous and the rich and the interests went to the ballot box to circumvent the legislature, they rarely bothered to provide funding to offset the new spending or tax reductions they demanded.

In the two decades beginning with Prop 98's passage in the spring of 1988, California voters considered 259 ballot measures. Of these, 127—nearly half—proposed something for nothing: that is, they increased spending or reduced taxes, or both, without offsetting funds. Of the 127 measures, 80, or about two-thirds, passed.

These something-for-nothing measures came in two types. Some were initiatives such as Proposition 70, a 1988 parks bond put together by Jerry Meral, then executive director of the Planning and Conservation League, the first of a series of initiatives he would write over the next fifteen years. Meral's passion was funding environmental and transportation projects that couldn't get over the supermajority budget hurdle in the legislature; his technique was "pay to play." Meral would go to local park supporters, businesses, real estate developers, and others and have them pony up signatures, dollars, or campaign workers in return for having their favored project or subsidy judged worthy by Meral of a place on an omnibus park or transportation funding initiative. His initiative bonds did not raise taxes to pay back the funds; they merely authorized a raid on the general fund.

Others soon organized their own raiding parties, including a 2004 measure to sell $3 billion in bonds to fund stem cell research and two children's hospital bond measures in 2004 and 2008. The children's hospitals, most of them private nonprofit organizations, left nothing to chance or state government discretion. In return for each hospital's putting up money for the campaign, each was written into the measure to receive a specified cut of the bond funds. On the day after voters approved the first bond, the campaign lawyer for the hospitals called the State Treasurer's Office and asked, "When do we get our money?"[13]

Liberals' causes weren't always the beneficiaries. Initiatives to promote expensive criminal justice policies, including the "three-strikes" sentencing law and the "Jessica's Law" restrictions on sex offenders, also required new general fund spending without identifying funding sources.

Other something-for-nothing measures were placed on the ballot by legislators themselves. Caught between the need to build schools, improve flood control, and relieve traffic congestion and the difficulty of rounding up a two-thirds vote for the taxes to pay for those things, lawmakers found it was easier to fund priorities by asking voters—through majority vote—to approve borrowing.

In this way, California turned the logic of requiring voter approval of debt on its head. The idea behind the requirement is that taking on public debt is the most serious fiscal decision a state makes. By issuing bonds, the state gives holders of the debt a claim on the state's revenues that takes priority over public safety and public health—indeed, over everything but schools. Moreover, debt taken out today is often repaid over long periods, sometimes into the next generation. The theory holds that such serious commitments require the people's direct consent.

But in California's system, voter approval of debt became the easy way out. Winning the majority approval of voters was far less difficult than winning a two-thirds vote in the legislature to raise taxes. If anything, the growing frustration with gridlock in the legislature seems to have emboldened Californians to vote for bonds. In the decade beginning with Prop 98 in 1988 and concluding with the elections of 1996, voters rejected about half as much in borrowing as they approved. In the second decade after Prop 98, ending with the elections in 2006, voters approved nearly five times as much debt as in the first decade, and rejected only two bond measures.

In 2007 the State Treasurer's Office took the measure of California's growing enthusiasm for debt. Assuming that voters would continue to approve new bonds over the next twenty years at the same rate that they had for the previous twenty years, it plotted the state's debt service for currently authorized bonds and new bonds into the future. It found that California would never have enough revenue to cover both core programs and the projected debt service. As long as California voters hew to their preference for something-for-nothing measures, the state's budget gap will persist.[14]

This embrace of something-for-nothing measures has created a new fiscal reality: California has two state budgets. One is passed by lawmakers, who must, under the state constitution, at least pretend to enact a balanced document. The other budget is improvised by voters at the ballot box and is under no such restriction. Over time, lawmakers have found the task of reconciling the voter-improvised, ballot-approved budget with their own budget to be an increasingly difficult task.

CLOSING DOWN THE SCHOOL
FOR POLITICS

Some initiatives robbed the legislature of power indirectly. The 1990 initiative to impose term limits on the legislature, Proposition 140, was a more direct attack. By the end of the decade, these tight new limits—no more than three terms (six years) in the Assembly and two terms (eight years) in the State Senate—would deprive the legislature of policy experience and weaken personal bonds between members. They would make it harder for the legislature to reckon with big issues—and leave even more of the field for the initiative process.

More than any single measure, Prop 140 closed the door on the "school for politics" that Sandy Muir had studied just fifteen years earlier. In his book, Muir had recounted a conversation in which veteran legislator Randy Collier schooled his new colleague Jerry Lewis about how to make a mark as a legislator:

> I assume you intend to stay around here and that you intend to do more than just get re-elected. I would hope, Jerry, that you will choose not to have answers to all the problems, that you will find maybe two or three problems which affect your district and go to work on them. Imagine that this wall is a huge mural. And you have a responsibility for part of that mural. You want to make a puzzle out of your part of it. Every bill you introduce is like a piece of that puzzle. You want to think five and ten years down the line so that, one piece at a time, that puzzle gets assembled.[15]

But under term limits no one had a decade to solve a complex legislative puzzle. No one could stay in one house of the legislature that long. So why bother to spend the time to become an expert if you were going to be gone by the time you knew anything? Before term limits, ascending to the chairmanship of a committee required a long apprenticeship. Under term limits, between one-third and one-half of Assembly members were, at all times, in their very first term in the legislature. Some of these freshmen were chairing committees. In 2003 the Assembly would elect a speaker, Fabian Núñez, who was in his very first term. In 2010 the Assembly did it again, choosing freshman John A. Pérez as speaker.

This legislative body of amateurs received less professional advice. Prop 140 dismantled much of the legislature's staff infrastructure by requiring cuts in legislative expenditures. Supporters of the initiative had wanted to force cuts in jobs for political aides. But state lawmakers, being politicians, instead cut from the staff many of the nonpartisan experts who provided institutional knowledge. The Legislative Analyst's Office lost more than a third of its staff after the passage of Prop 140. The Assembly Office of Research was eventually shut.[16]

Term limits boosted turnover and may have increased the percentage of women and minorities serving in the legislature. But this more racially diverse cast of politicians occupied a badly weakened institution. Campaign finance limits, also approved by the voters, undermined the legislative leadership that remained. Top officials in the Assembly and Senate, before new campaign regulations, had been able to maintain central control of election donations and amass huge stockpiles. Muir disliked this dynamic, but allowed that "there were times when all the powers of the Speaker seemed vitally necessary."[17] When individual lawmakers would try to bully colleagues by defying the rules, or shake down other lawmakers or lobbyists, or attempt to take each other's bills hostage, the strong legislative leaders of the past could quickly put a stop to it.

The discipline forced by legislative leaders was particularly important on difficult, high-profile votes on the budget. A lawmaker who crossed the leadership on such a vote risked his career. But under campaign contribution limits, with donations limited to a few thousand dollars per donor, individual members raised more of their own money, and leaders held less sway. It was harder to get things done without the discipline that a well-funded leadership provided. And, with individual members having to devote more hours to fund-raising, there was less time to get things done.

"With all this campaign reform and the distrust by the public of the legislative process, it's not as much fun up here as before," said the late legislator Al Alquist in an oral history. Term limits did not destroy the political class of career politicians. Instead they spent more of their time politicking, playing musical chairs as they jumped between state and local offices. Many of the new members were staffers or relatives of previous members. Alquist's own wife, Elaine, took his seat, first in the Assembly, then in the Senate. "I tell all my friends that I'm her chief consultant, that she only pays me a dollar a year because she can't put me on the state payroll," Alquist would say. "But the fringe benefits that go with the job are pretty good."[18]

THE CYCLE OF CONTEMPT

Term limits produced more politicking and undermined expertise in all fifteen state legislatures upon which they have been imposed. But in California, term limits were even more destructive because of how they combined with other features of the state's governing system. Term limits helped complete a cycle of contempt that weakened the legislature while strengthening the initiative process.

In part because they didn't trust legislators, voters slowly took power away from lawmakers and increasingly required them to decide issues by supermajority consensus, or under laws imposed by initiative. Hamstrung, legislators had less success in taking decisive action on difficult issues, especially fiscal decisions that required a two-thirds vote. More and more, they delivered muddled compromises that pleased voters on neither side of controversial issues, or they resorted to tricks and borrowing. Voters, angry at this, passed more initiatives and took more matters into their own hands, deepening the state's fiscal hole. Confined to the sidelines on many policy matters, state lawmakers served as cleanup crew for the budget mess voters made.

Take prisons. By passing "three strikes" and other "tough" crime measures, voters had given a big push to a more than fivefold increase in the state's prison population over the twenty-year period beginning in 1982. Annual state spending on prisons more than doubled in the first decade of the twenty-first century. Lawmakers were boxed in. If they wanted to send fewer people to prison, they would have to find ways around the voter-approved sentencing laws. If they built more prisons, they would have to get around voter-approved limits on taxation. Unable to reach consensus, lawmakers failed to act, forcing the federal courts to step in and demand changes. Even under pressure from the courts, legislators managed only to find some short-term savings, release some prisoners, and push the problem into the future.

In this and so many other matters, the legislature served a useful purpose: as a scapegoat. Californians were always unhappy with their legislature. They berated it on talk radio, mocked it in online comments and letters to the editor, and disapproved of it when the pollsters called. As state government hurtled toward insolvency in mid-2009, voter approval of the legislature's performance fell to 14 percent, the low-water mark in the nearly three decades the Field Poll has been taking such soundings. What might be done? Many voters, rather than restoring greater expertise to the body, instead supported an initiative to weaken the legislature further by making it a part-time body.

And so the cycle of contempt rolls on.

Voters didn't recognize that they might be responsible for their own unhappiness. The last time more voters approved of the legislature than disapproved of it was shortly before they voted in term limits. Over thirty years, voters slowly squeezed the life out of their legislature but never stopped complaining that it didn't work. Californians in this way resemble nothing so much as the boy who murders his mother and then complains that he's an orphan.

PART II
THE CALIFORNIA FIX

5

BUDGETING WITHOUT SHACKLES

How does California extract itself from its self-imposed calamity?

For many Californians, the way out starts (and for some Californians ends) with money and budgets. And with good reason. The contrast between California as an economy—rich and dynamic—and California as public fiscal manager is too stark to ignore. California has been an economic powerhouse of the Information Age, driving key sectors of the national economy into the future—information technology, software, communications, biotech, entertainment. It has also been, with increasing frequency, a fiscal wreck.

State budget emergencies have rolled in, one after another, like the breakers at Huntington Beach. In 1983, during George Deukmejian's first year as governor and with the "obscene surplus" still fresh in Californians' memories, the state came within a few days of not being able to pay its bills. Deukmejian later bragged in his successful 1986 reelection campaign that he had taken California "from IOU to A-OK." But by 1990, his final year in office, with the state plunging again into a deep deficit, capitol wags rewrote Deukmejian's trajectory to read, "from IOU to A-OK to Oh, sh**."

The crisis he bequeathed to his successor, Pete Wilson, consumed Wilson's first term and forced the state briefly, in the summer of 1992, to issue IOUs. After a few heady years of the Internet stock market bubble in the late 1990s, big deficits returned in 2002. They have ever since been a permanent feature of California life, reaching unprecedented depths in 2009, when the state was forced to halt all infrastructure projects and send out IOUs to contractors awaiting payments and taxpayers awaiting refunds.[1] When recessions strike, other states also sing the fiscal blues; the revenue collapse of 2008–10, the worst since the Great Depression, created budget deficits in forty-two states in 2009. But in no other state have budget crises been as deep, as frequent in both good economic years and bad, and as politically intractable as in California. Between 1989 and 2008, the legislature managed only five times to pass a budget before the July 1 beginning of the fiscal year.[2]

BUDGETING BY HEAVY METAL

If the nation's richest state has come to have the nation's lowest credit rating, it is not for lack of constitutional efforts to impose fiscal discipline on government. California is America's house of budget bondage.

Its constitutional closet is packed full of budget whips, shackles, and chains. No other state binds its governors and legislatures with such an array of fiscal fetters.[3] There is the familiar two-thirds majority vote requirement for passing budgets and nonschool appropriations. And the two-thirds vote requirement for revenue increases. And the state spending limit. And the balanced budget rule. And the rainy-day fund in which money must be set aside in good times. And the limits on borrowing, both in the financial markets and from transportation accounts and local government. And the Proposition 98 funding guarantee for schools and community colleges. And as we have seen, in addition to these direct controls, California permits voters, through the initiative, to conduct a second budget process limiting the discretion of elected officials. California voters have used that power vigorously to create spending obligations for health, mental health, prisons, drug treatment, environmental protection, parks, early childhood education, and after-school programs, mandates that often cannot be altered except with the voters' approval.

Again and again, California voters have been told that some fiscal outcomes are too vital to leave to the ordinary push and pull of legislative budgeting and democratic politics—so vital, in fact, that they must be locked into the constitution. Over and over, they have been told that, without constitutional mandates that tell lawmakers how much to spend on education and supermajority rules on tax and spending bills, schools would crumble and taxes would soar. California voters have often taken that advice to heart.

So the questions naturally arise. Why does California, with the most rigid constitutional budget rules and the most extensive supermajority voting requirements, have the nation's longest-running fiscal mess? Could it be that all the restraints don't work? Could it be that they actually make things worse?

CHAINED TO IRRESPONSIBILITY: SPENDING

To measure the effectiveness of California's budget shackles, let's start by testing a hypothesis. If the budget restraints enacted in California over the past several decades had worked as advertised, we would expect the conservatives who championed most of them to be happy with California's fiscal direction, wouldn't we?

They are not. No other group is so noisily dismayed by the results of California's experiment in budget bondage. Five years after Governor Arnold Schwarzenegger promised in the 2003 recall campaign to end California's "crazy deficit spending," years in which he himself submitted a budget to the legislature and then wielded a line-item veto pen over the final version passed by a supermajority of lawmakers, Schwarzenegger was still complaining, "We do not have a revenue problem; we have a spending problem."[4] Republican legislators agreed. "It's time for lawmakers and the Governor to once and for all address the root of our budget problems—years of overspending," said Assemblyman Roger Niello, formerly vice chair of the Assembly Budget Committee.[5] Conservative politicians and bloggers constantly complain that Californians pay "some of the highest taxes." They repeat the phrase so often and so exactly that it must be programmed into their computers. If you take what conservatives say at face value, the nation's strictest regime of constitutional budget constraints has failed to deliver what they hoped.

It would easy to accept conservatives' judgment on the subject—and given their continuing and strenuous devotion to the very budget restraints whose outcomes they decry, it would be wickedly fun as well. But as one California conservative, Richard Nixon, once famously said, it would be wrong. Political words are rarely meant to illuminate; they are weapons, wielded to spur action and seize advantage. Hostility to taxes and government spending is the strong force that holds together the Republican coalition. At a time when conservatives are at odds with a majority of Californians on environmental regulation, climate change, transportation priorities, education spending, and abortion, it is the issue that gives them the greatest political traction with the wider electorate.[6] For them to admit that California's panoply of budget restraints has actually lowered spending and taxes would be to surrender a key issue.

A better test of California's shackles is to look at what has happened to California's finances since the era of constraints began in earnest in 1978 with the passage of Prop 13. The picture is not pretty. Instead of promoting fiscal responsibility, budget constraints have mainly served to push California deeper into debt.

When it comes to spending, California's constitution wears both belts and suspenders: it sports both a spending limit and the two-thirds requirement for passage of the budget. Neither has made much difference. State general fund spending, measured as a share of the state's personal income, has moved in a narrow range over the past three decades, reaching a low point in 2009–10 because of cuts forced by the Great Recession (see Figure 1). The combined spending of state and local governments in Cali-

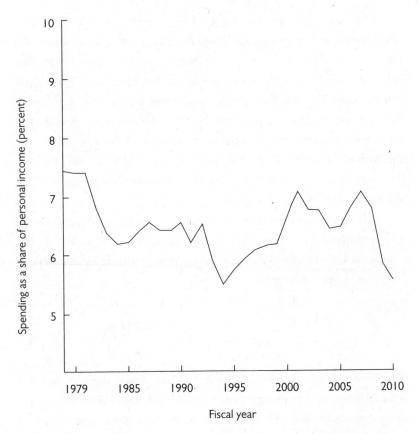

Figure 1 General Fund Spending in California, 1979–2010. *Source:* Legislative Analyst's Office, California Department of Finance."

fornia has grown at about the same rate as in the average state, and in many cases more than in states that have no spending limits or two-thirds vote requirements for the budget and taxes.[7]

That should come as no surprise. Academic research has shown that supermajority requirements for budgets either fail to reduce spending or actually increase it.[8] California's experience with the two-thirds majority rule follows that pattern.

Consider what happened, for example, in the summer of 2001, when the Republican minority held up the state budget for weeks in a fight over a quarter-cent sales tax triggered by a growing deficit. Governor Gray Davis and Democratic leaders in the legislature eventually won the votes of a handful of Central Valley Republican legislators by offering expanded aid to rural law enforcement and tax breaks to growers and timber operators. One prominent conservative legislator in California, the former state senator and now U.S. Representative Tom McClintock, broke with his party to acknowledge the problem: "The two-thirds vote for the budget has not contained spending, and it blurs accountability."[9] Time and again, lawmakers have used the two-thirds vote rule to leverage more money for their districts.

"Although conventional wisdom indicates otherwise, the two-thirds vote requirement does not seem to limit higher levels of spending," the California Constitutional Revision Commission wrote in its 1996 report. "In practice, it encourages it."[10]

CHAINED TO IRRESPONSIBILITY: TAXES

Taxes are a different story. California's constitutional shackles on taxes have reduced the overall state and local tax burden on California taxpayers, a result consistent with the findings of academic research on supermajority tax-vote requirements in the states.[11] In 1977, the year before Prop 13 was passed, Californians paid 15 percent more of their personal income in state and local taxes than the national average, and California ranked behind only Alaska, New York, Massachusetts, and Vermont in tax burden. By 2006, California's tax burden had fallen to only 4 percent more than the national average and its rank to fourteenth among the states.

California's retreat from the ranks of high-tax states was powered mainly by the property tax cuts in Prop 13. California has gone from having one of the highest property tax burdens to one of the lowest. But it is also driven by Prop 13's provision requiring a two-thirds vote in each house of the legislature for any revenue increase.

That provision created "the Ratchet." Combined with the supermajority rule on budgets, Prop 13 has given anti-tax conservatives an effective veto over state fiscal policy, despite their having been in the minority for all but two of the thirty-two years since Prop 13 passed. They have used that veto to block tax increases and ratchet down the state's tax base at every opportunity by demanding tax breaks for favored industries or activities, as in the 2001 giveaway to rural legislators.

The Ratchet was cranked most furiously during the dot-com bubble of the late 1990s. Flush with revenue, California cut the corporate tax, the income tax, and most precipitously, the vehicle license fee, the property tax on vehicles that the state had been collecting on behalf of local governments since 1935. When the bubble burst and the hot money evaporated, the ratcheted-down tax base could no longer support the existing base of public services. The Ratchet, however, turns one way only: Revenue reduced by majority vote can only be restored by supermajorities, which rarely materialize. And the Ratchet keeps turning even in the worst of times. In February 2009, with the state on the verge of issuing IOUs, the price of obtaining a handful of Republican votes for a $40 billion budget fix, which contained temporary tax increases, was a permanent $2 billion-a-year tax cut for large multistate corporations.[12]

CHAINED TO IRRESPONSIBILITY: DEBT

Every time California's unique budget shackles yield a huge new budget deficit, the response of the state's leaders is to place an order for a new set of chains. In 2004, Schwarzenegger and legislative leaders asked voters to approve Proposition 58, "The California Balanced Budget Act," a constitutional amendment to require a balanced budget, create an $8 billion rainy-day reserve fund, and prohibit *future* borrowing to cover over deficits. The key word here is "future." On the same ballot they also sought and won voter consent for Proposition 57 to borrow $15 billion to cover the state's budget deficit, much of it the result of the tax cuts of the prior decade. "Combined, the two measures will allow California to refinance its debt and prevent such a situation from EVER HAPPENING AGAIN," Schwarzenegger wrote in the voter information guide (emphasis in original).

The measures prevented nothing. Despite Prop 58, the state spent about $26 billion more than it received in revenues in the first decade of the twenty-first century. In budget after budget, Schwarzenegger looked to skate around the Prop 58 prohibition on borrowing with new gimmicks and deferrals: pension obligation bonds, borrowing against future tribal gaming revenues, borrowing from hoped-for increases in future lottery revenues—the last a device he once described as "gifts from the future." In 2008 he sold $3 billion of the Prop 57 deficit bonds that were passed with the promise to voters that they would be used for the 2004 crisis and never again. With the two-thirds rule blocking legislative approval of higher user fees, California's traditional method of financing infrastructure such as roads, the state turned to using general obligation bonds. By July 2009, Legislative Analyst Mac Taylor estimated the state had accumulated liabilities of about $200 billion, or twice the annual general fund budget, in budget debt, infrastructure borrowing, and unfunded retirement benefits. All this debt was piled up in California's era of budget bondage.[13]

CHAINED TO MEDIOCRITY:
PROP 98

If the results of applying the conservatives' budget shackles have been less than satisfactory, either to conservatives themselves or to the state as a whole, what about the left's favorite straitjacket: the Prop 98 minimum funding guarantee for schools and community colleges? Are liberals and educators, Prop 98's creators and its most fervent advocates, any happier with the results of their measure?

No, they are not. "California continues to lag behind the national average in per pupil funding, has some of the largest class sizes in the country and ranks dead last in the number of counselors and librarians in our schools," says the California Teachers Association (CTA).

"We would have to increase our spending by almost $2,400 per student—or 31 percent—simply to reach the national average," Jack O'Connell, California's superintendent of public instruction, said in his 2009 State of Education Address. "Keep in mind," he added, "this ranking was done before the current budget cuts were calculated." Paula S. Campbell, president of the California School Boards Association, described those deep cuts in school funding for 2009–10, which were fully consistent with the terms of Prop 98, as "worse than a retreat; it is a massacre."[14]

In the case of school funding, the hyperbole is grounded in fact. Prop 98 has been no match for the effects of Prop 13 and the Ratchet.

A generation ago, California was among the nation's leaders in school support. When the tax revolt hit, it was spending about $600 more per pupil than the national average. In the wake of Prop 13, that support fell sharply relative to spending in the rest of the nation, to about $100 per pupil above average in 1988, the year voters passed Prop 98. But passage of the initiative did not break the trend; within a decade California spending had fallen to more than $600 per pupil below the national average (all figures are in constant 1999–2000 dollars). California played catch-up in the years of the Internet stock bubble, when the legislature briefly boosted school spending above the Prop 98 minimum guarantee. It lagged again after the stock market bust, when Governor Schwarzenegger and the legislature suspended Prop 98.

Education experts use different yardsticks to compare school funding levels: per pupil spending, per pupil spending adjusted for state costs (California's are higher because its more productive workforce commands higher-than-average wages), and school funding as a percentage of personal income. But none of these measures provides any evidence that Prop 98 has moved California toward the head of the school-funding pack. "When adjusted for cost differences across states, California's spending is lower than that of Texas, Florida, New York, and the rest of the country as a whole," a comprehensive review of California school finances reported in 2007.[15]

That unhappy record has triggered a debate among analysts. Does

Prop 98 actually restrict school spending instead of propping it up? The CTA vigorously disputes that. But the vigor and frequency of its proclamation that Prop 98 is a floor, not a ceiling, remind you of the used-car salesman who repeatedly says that the unmatched paint on the car's fender is only a cosmetic flaw and no sign of a past wreck.[16]

There is no denying, however, that Prop 98 has changed the politics of school finance in ways that have been bad for both schools and democracy in California. The key question in school funding is whether we are spending the right amount on the right things to get the level of student achievement the state needs. Since the passage of Prop 98, California rarely asks that question.

Instead, lawmakers, the governor, and the education lobby wrestle over Prop 98 technical questions that make the heads of ordinary mortals ache: for instance, if revenue shortfalls put the state into a Test 1 year, does that create a maintenance factor? They sometimes argue, in bad times, about whether to suspend Prop 98, and in good times about whether to overfund it. But mostly they don't argue over the things that matter to the schools.

Prop 98 is the default position in California politics. Politically, it is a safe harbor; we do not know of a single politician who has lost an election because he or she declined to overfund the Prop 98 minimum guarantee. Indeed, because any funds appropriated to the schools in excess of the guarantee get built into the Prop 98 base in future years, creating new budget obligations and potential future budget trouble, Prop 98 makes it risky for any politician to spend more on schools than the minimum required. Prop 98 has locked California schools into funding mediocrity and substandard achievement while muting the state's ability to debate the ways to improve them.

Given this track record—budgets perennially late and unbalanced, IOUs and expanding state debt, underfunded and underperforming schools—it's hard not to conclude that the sellers of budget whips and chains have been peddling a scam. But the worst thing about budget shackles is not that they are bad fiscal policy. The worst thing, as we will see now, is that they are profoundly undemocratic.

UNDERMINING DEMOCRACY

Californians see, hear, and read lots of reporting and commentary about the state budget. They hear when the budget is late. They hear when the budget is unbalanced. They hear about spending and tax levels. But they rarely hear that some Californians' priorities carried twice as much weight in passing the budget as those of their neighbors. Yet that is precisely the result of California's various supermajority requirements and budget mandates. Even if the two-thirds rules could be shown to reliably produce certain policy results, such as lower state spending or taxes, they would still have no legitimate place in the state constitution because they undermine the fundamental premise of a democratic society: that every citizen has an equal say.

Most of us take pride in the central thread of America's history, and California's: the long march to full and equal political participation by all, a march that has left behind, as relics of an imperfect and embarrassing past, the former voting restrictions based on property, race, and gender. Few Americans dissent from what the political scientist Robert Dahl calls the two fundamental judgments underlying our democracy: the moral judgment that each person is of intrinsic equal worth; and the practical judgment that, in governing public affairs, each person is a better judge of his or her interests and preferences than any aristocracy or elite that pretends to greater knowledge of the common good. As a nation, we have often made the promotion of democracy abroad a central tenet of our foreign policy. It is, therefore, both surprising and troubling that California's media and leaders pay so little attention to the most objectionable feature of California's budgeting: that it is deeply undemocratic.[17]

The U.S. Constitution written in Philadelphia in 1787 may now fall short of modern democratic standards, but its framers at least seem to have understood the nature of democracy better than many present-day Californians. They considered, but rejected, proposals to require super-majority votes in Congress for budgets and ordinary legislation, reserving two-thirds votes for the approval of constitutional amendments, conviction in an impeachment trial, ratification of treaties, and the override of a presidential veto. Writing in Federalist 58 in 1788, founder James Madison explained how the disadvantages of supermajority votes outweigh any potential advantages: "In all cases where Justice or the general good might require new laws to be passed, or active measures to be pursued, the fundamental principle of free government would be reversed." he wrote. "It would be no longer the majority that would rule: the power would be transferred to the minority."[18]

Under California's budget rules, that minority can be very small. It takes only one-third plus one of the members in either house of the legislature to block a budget or a revenue increase. As we will see in Chapter 6, it doesn't require a majority of the electorate to create a majority legislative party; it takes even fewer votes to produce a minority veto and control the state's fiscal direction. And this undemocratic minority veto is not, in California, limited to budget priorities. Determined minorities can also use the two-thirds rule on fiscal matters to leverage passage or to defeat totally unrelated measures, as Madison anticipated two centuries ago. "An interested minority might take advantage of it to screen themselves from equitable sacrifices to the general weal," he warned, "or, in particular emergencies, to extort unreasonable indulgences."[19]

In the early 2009 fiscal emergency, for example, with the state running out of cash, Assembly Republicans not only vowed to oppose any budget fix that included temporary tax increases; they also insisted on a whole range of changes to California law, including reducing the wage-and-hour protections of workers, limiting citizens' ability to seek redress in civil lawsuits against businesses that had harmed them, changing rules on disabled access to public places, and permitting polluters to delay cleanup of dirty diesel engines responsible for the high rate of lung and heart disease in many parts of the state. Their wish list went unanswered, but

State Senator Abel Maldonado, as the price of his vote for the budget, was able to extract passage of a constitutional amendment, never considered in committee and highly unlikely to have won legislative approval on its own merits, to abolish party primaries in California and substitute a form of election known as a "top two" or "jungle" primary. California law explicitly bars this kind of logrolling, which was worth roughly $2 million dollars to Maldonado in forgone costs of trying to qualify his amendment for the ballot as an initiative. But the police did not show up on the senator's doorstep. As Madison understood, supermajority rules make such abuses of democracy inevitable, and in California so commonplace that we have lost our sense of outrage.[20]

UNJUSTIFIABLE VETO

"A requirement for a super majority—that is, a minority veto—must be justified by an explicit principle that is itself justifiable," Robert Dahl writes. No one has ever convincingly offered such a principle for California's uniquely undemocratic budget rules.[21]

Many conservatives say the two-thirds requirement for passing budgets and appropriations is necessary to protect against higher government spending. As we've seen, its real effect has been to raise spending. But even if the current rule actually had the effect they say they desire, the rule is far broader than needed to achieve that result. The minority veto in California doesn't apply only to higher spending; it applies to passage of any budget or any appropriation, even if it reduces spending. At the same time, the rule is too narrow to achieve overall spending control. It applies neither to school appropriations, which can be approved by a majority of legislators, nor to ballot initiatives, which by vote of a simple majority give voters the power to spend to their heart's content. A supermajority requirement for spending votes that applies only to the legislature but not to the people themselves is not a principle. It is constitutional Viagra for those whose electoral performance leaves them in need of the boost provided by a minority veto.

That is equally true of the Prop 98 minimum school-funding guarantee, which can be suspended only through a vote by a supermajority of lawmakers. No high principle lies behind it. Most Californians agree that good schools and community colleges are vital to the state's future success; they disagree about how much money is needed to achieve that result. In a real democracy, citizens would debate the issue and then vote their choices. Not in California. Prop 98 embeds into the constitution the school funding level preferred by a majority of voters in 1988. Is their choice the right answer for today's California? As long as Prop 98 is in the constitution, it's pointless to ask. Prop 98 makes it possible for a minority of lawmakers to force on today's California the opinions held by California voters two decades ago, and it makes that outcome almost inevitable. Respecting one's elders is a fine thing, but rule by ancestors is not democracy.

On the tax side of the equation, two arguments are often offered to justify the supermajority vote requirement in the legislature to raise revenue.

In the first, conservatives argue that raising taxes is of such consequence to the economy that it should be made more difficult. But it takes only a quick look at the international and state data on taxation levels and per capita income to see that there is no direct relationship between taxes and economic success. Low taxes haven't made Alabama or Mexico rich, high taxes haven't made New York or Sweden poor. Moreover, liberals often argue the opposite—that high levels of public investment in education and infrastructure are necessary for growth. These are choices for voters to make, not principles that justify a departure from democracy to give a minority the power to impose its particular view.

The second argument, from a libertarian perspective, holds that a supermajority vote requirement is essential to protect individuals and particular groups against having their property taxed to support public purposes. A simple majority shouldn't be able to impose a public obligation on a subset of citizens. But it is hard to see why tax decisions should be treated differently in a democracy than the other public decisions that legislatures make. They often choose by majority vote to make many choices that weigh heavily on individual persons and their property, and on subsets of the larger society: what vegetation they may smoke, whom they can marry, when they can divorce, how much they can recover in lawsuits for harms done to them, and whether they can use their land as a toxic waste dump. And in any event, most of those who support the two-thirds rule on taxes do not subscribe to it consistently. Have you ever heard a libertarian argue that replacing California's progressive income tax with a flat tax should require a two-thirds majority in the legislature because it would raise the taxes on some subgroups (low- and middle-income households) even as it lowers them for others (the rich)?

BUDGETING WITHOUT SHACKLES

If Californians were to decide to throw off these undemocratic straitjackets, what should a more responsible and more democratic fiscal system look like?

For all of California's partisan divisions, there is a broad consensus across the political spectrum on the goals of fiscal reform. A new California budget system should be simpler and more transparent, with honest accounting to keep policy makers from hiding deficits. It should yield spending plans that are balanced, not only in the short run, but also in the long run, so that today's obligations are not dumped onto future taxpayers. It should be flexible enough to meet new public needs as they arise, adjust quickly to changing voter priorities, and deal with the inevitable ups and downs of the economy. It should encourage efficient delivery of public services. It should be responsive to voters' priorities and assure them that, from the state capitol to city halls, they can hold elected officials accountable for their fiscal performance.

Fortunately, California has no shortage of good ideas to draw on to help the state meet those goals. For more than a decade, various commissions, public finance experts, and nonprofit groups have been churning out sensible recommendations. Other states offer models of prudent fiscal management that can be readily copied. Here is an outline for fixing California's broken fiscal system:

1. Start with budget accounting that tells the truth. Not only does California routinely fail to balance its budget; it can't even talk straight about its finances. Getting the accounting and presentation correct isn't just a cosmetic nicety. Voters and policy makers can't make good decisions if they don't know the state's real financial circumstances.

No one understands this better than former governor Davis. In 2003 he hyped the size of the state's budget problem, talking incessantly about a $38 billion "shortfall." He apparently believed that the bigger the stated challenge, the more likely California would be to act on it. He was half right. Californians were indeed appalled by the size of the "shortfall." Unfortunately for Davis, they ignored his proposed solutions and instead recalled him for having let the problem grow so large.

Budgets don't have to be hard to understand. In normal accounting and common understanding, your annual budget is balanced if you spend only as much as you earn. If revenues are greater than spending, the difference is a surplus; if spending exceeds revenues, the difference is a deficit.

But not in California. When California's state government runs into budget problems, leaders (and the press) variously and promiscuously refer to them as a "shortfall," a "hole," a "gap," and a "deficit." Imagine a citizen who scoured the news in early 2008 to learn about the state's fiscal situation. She would have read that California had an "$8 billion budget shortfall" (*San Jose Mercury News*), "a $10 billon gap" (*Sacramento Bee*), or a budget "$20 billion out of whack" (*San Diego Union-Tribune*)—"out of whack" being Arnold Schwarzenegger's linguistic contribution to budget clarity. If this same citizen had closed down her browser feeling disoriented by the cacophony of numbers and nouns, it would have been with good reason—she was being badly served by both her government and the news media.

Sometimes the numbers and nouns in the news actually refer to the real deficit, the amount by which spending exceeds revenue in the year.

More often than not, though, they are referring to an amalgam of a kind found nowhere else in accounting. They add up the amount of the state's cash reserve at the beginning of the current year, the amount by which spending will exceed revenue in the current year (the deficit), the projected deficit in the coming budget year, and the amount of cash policy makers want to have in the kitty when the coming year ends. As UCLA professor Daniel Mitchell and his late colleague Werner Z. Hirsch have repeatedly pointed out, California's bad habit of talking about this "shortfall" combines a stock of money (your savings account) with two flows (your salary and your bills), obscuring the state's true fiscal situation.[22]

Most people understand that if they earn $50,000 in a year but spend $100,000, they won't balance their household budget by drawing down their savings account or running up charges on their credit card. California doesn't. Even if it spends more than it collects in taxes, California government counts the budget as balanced if it can find the cash, from reserves or by borrowing, to make up the difference. That's why the state's leaders so often proclaim that the state has a balanced budget right up to the day California goes broke and sends out IOUs.

California is also confused about the meaning of "revenues." Asked at a 2008 budget conference whether Schwarzenegger would consider raising revenues to balance the budget, Thomas Sheehy, deputy director of the Department of Finance, replied that the governor's budget, in fact, already included new revenues: $3.3 billion from the sale of deficit bonds! A corporate executive who reports borrowed dollars as sales is angling for a bunk in federal prison. It doesn't take much financial sophistication to understand that a cash advance on your credit card isn't revenue. It is debt. And so, of course, is California's borrowing to cover up deficits. When the top people in the state's finance department think debt is revenue, you know California's fiscal problems go all the way to the bone.

The first, crucial step toward responsible and democratic budgeting is to present the state's fiscal information to Californians honestly and clearly. Spending is the amount the state pays for goods, services, and

interest, and for grants it makes to individuals and other levels of government. Revenue is the proceeds of taxes, fees, interest on investments, and
transfers from other levels of government if they do not require repayment. Money borrowed from the public or other levels of government, if
it requires repayment and is not to be repaid within the budget year, is
debt, not revenue. Determining whether the budget for the year is balanced is no more complicated than subtracting spending from revenue.
This format, identical to that used by the federal government, provides
policy makers and the public alike exactly the information they need to
understand California's fiscal situation and make decisions about changing course.[23]

2. *Create a real rainy-day fund.* An honest presentation of state finances
would put California in position to take the big second step: to begin
honestly balancing its budget over time. This requires actions a little
more complicated than the sound-bite cry for the state "to live within its
means" but no more complex than the kind of prudent financial planning households do.

California, like other states, needs to balance its budget because the
alternative is too expensive. State government must regularly go into the
financial markets to borrow money. Sometimes the state needs to borrow
short-term cash within a budget year to fill in the gaps between when
it spends budgeted funds and when tax payments arrive; think of this
borrowing as a kind of payday loan. Sometimes the state sells long-term
bonds to finance the construction of capital projects like schools and prisons; think of this borrowing as a mortgage. The price California pays in
interest for both kinds of borrowing depends on investors' judgment of
the risk of not being repaid in full or on time. For most of the first decade
of this century, as California ran persistent budget deficits and finally, in
2009, resorted to IOUs to pay some bills, the price was very high: California had the lowest credit rating among the states and ended up paying
high interest rates that cost taxpayers tens of millions more than it would
have if the state were more prudently managed. Indeed, at the bottom

of the 2007–09 recession, investors judged California so risky that they briefly stopped lending to the state at any price, which cut off funding of infrastructure projects at the very moment Californians most needed the investment and jobs.

In a world with no business cycles, the state could assure itself of ready and affordable access to credit by hewing to a decree of biblical simplicity: thou shalt balance thy revenue and thy spending in each and every year. In the real world, where the cycle of boom and bust in the economy leads to ever wilder swings in revenue collections, the fundamentalist mandate to always balance revenue and spending would yield equally wild swings in state policy. California would spend and cut taxes like mad in good years to take advantage of the revenue flood. And it would cut spending and raise taxes like mad in bad years, at the very moment when those actions would deepen a downturn. In good years it would spend money to better train young teachers and build new college campuses. Then, when the next downturn arrived, it would lay off the young teachers it had just expensively trained and limit enrollment at the campuses it had just built. Turning public services on and off to the beat of the business cycle doesn't make for good or efficient government. Yet it is exactly how California is now operating.

The less biblical but more commonsense solution is to balance the budget over the business cycle. That is how prudent households behave. They don't run a balanced budget every year. In most years they spend less than they earn. In the other years, either because their earnings fall as a result of retirement or job loss, or because they must make a major purchase, such as a car, a house, or a college education, they spend more than they earn by drawing on their savings. They balance their budgets over a lifetime.

To create a state government version of prudent household budgeting, California needs a robust and well-disciplined rainy-day fund to replace the two leaky reserves it now has. One, the Special Fund for Economic Uncertainties, is little more than a checking account where revenues in excess of the budget forecast are stashed until the legislature and the governor get around to spending them. The other, the badly designed Budget Stabilization Account created by Prop 58 in 2004, has been a fiscal flop. Capped at $8 billion, or 5 percent of projected general fund revenues, it's too small to deal with the much larger revenue swings the state has experienced in the past three recessions. It requires the state to squirrel away 3 percent of revenues every year, without regard to California's budget or economic condition, but allows the governor to withhold all or part of the annual contribution, for any reason.[24] And it allows up to half of the money in the account to be spent, whether it's rainy or sunny.

A better rainy-day fund would be large enough—at least 15 percent of the state budget—to keep state services on an even keel in a typical recession. It would be funded by automatic transfers of all revenues collected in excess of the budgeted amount for the year and all projected revenues sharply in excess of the average growth of the previous ten years, with the averages adjusted for any tax cuts or tax increases. The funds could be withdrawn and spent only in years when revenues are projected (or actually turn out) to be significantly lower than the average growth of the prior ten years, and then only in amounts by which revenue collections fall short of that average. Exceptions would be allowed only for true emergencies, such as wars and earthquakes. Most states use at least one of these rules to reduce the amount of budget pain in bad times.[25]

The words "sharply" and "significantly" are deliberately vague. The goal ought to be a state budget that hugs the long-term trend line of economic growth in California and does not intensify the pain of downturns by piling on big spending cuts and tax increases of the kind the legislature was forced to enact in 2009 at the depths of the Great Recession. But just how closely the budget needs to hug that line is a decision to make democratically and with an eye to leaving enough flexibility for leaders and citizens to meet changing circumstances.

3. Pay as you go. Even with straightforward accounting and an adequate rainy-day fund, state government could still dig itself into a budget hole.

Like all those wanna-be homeowners during the housing bubble—the ones who used a low teaser rate to qualify for a bigger house than they could afford, then went into foreclosure once the mortgage adjusted—governments have a bad habit of committing to policy changes that are affordable today but come with balloon payments in what budget wonks call the "out years."

California today lives in the "out years" of the dot-com stock market boom of the late 1990s, when the California state government threw a party it has yet to recover from. From capital gains and Silicon Valley stock options—"the greatest legal creation of wealth in the history of the planet," John Doerr, the celebrated venture capitalist, called the Internet boom—the money poured in faster than the legislature and two governors, Wilson and Davis, could pump it out. They approved increases in spending. They cut taxes for individuals and corporations. Some of the higher spending was one shot, for highway projects and lower tuition at public universities, creating no enduring budget obligations. The cut in the vehicle license fee, as originally passed in 1998, was also meant to be automatically reversed if state revenues receded and Sacramento was no longer able to backfill cities and counties for the money they had lost. (But Arnold Schwarzenegger had other ideas, making the cut permanent after the 2003 recall of Gray Davis and putting a permanent hole in the state's budget.) Some of their revelry, however—including lower personal and corporate income taxes, smaller classes in schools, expanded college scholarship grants, and bigger Medi-Cal payments to doctors and nursing home operators—put permanent dents in the state's fiscal furniture. After the stock bubble burst in 2001 and the hot money vanished from the tax collector's till, the budget was in shambles.[26]

Had a strong rainy-day fund been in place in California in the years of the tech boom, it would have put a partial damper on the partying by diverting some of the intoxicating surge of revenue to future years. But a rainy-day fund is no guard against budget policy choices that, like acorns, start small and grow to fill the sky. Such a fund would have been no match for the classic case of an ever-expanding spending choice:

the decision by Davis and the legislature, in the midst of that boom, to enact SB 400, raising state worker pensions to the highest levels in the country.

In September 1999, overwhelming bipartisan majorities in both houses accepted, without debate, the assurances of the Davis administration and the California Public Employees' Retirement System (CalPERS) that bigger pensions would put no added pressure on the budget. CalPERS "anticipate[s] that the state's contribution to CalPERS will remain below the 1998–99 fiscal year for at least the next decade," legislators were told, with the higher payouts to current and future retirees coming out of the pension fund's bubble-swollen investment kitty.[27] But by 2003, after the dot-com bubble burst and a large share of the pension fund's value evaporated, state pension contributions as a share of payroll had tripled.

"If I had known, if anybody had known, that the market was going to tank for three years, and our contribution was going to go up the way it is, sure we wouldn't have done it," said Marty Morgenstern, the state personnel director who negotiated the pension increase, a few weeks before his boss was recalled in October 2003. Of course, a lot of people did know—from Federal Reserve Chairman Alan Greenspan, with his warnings of "irrational exuberance," to famed investor Warren Buffett, who spent the summer of 1999 telling anyone who would listen not to expect the bull market to continue for another seventeen years. But California's leaders wanted to believe. The tooth fairy had visited Sacramento, arm in arm with Santa Claus, and there was no budget process in place to test what that belief might cost in the future if it proved wrong.[28]

Preventing this kind of shortsightedness and wishful thinking requires taking a third big step toward responsible budgeting: adopting the discipline of pay-as-you-go.

Known to the fiscal cognoscenti as PAYGO, pay-as-you-go budgeting proved its mettle at the federal level in the 1990s. Congress put PAYGO into law as part of the 1990 deal with President George H. W. Bush to begin erasing the enormous federal deficits that were the legacy of the Reagan years. The PAYGO law required any tax cuts or legislated increases in entitlement programs like Social Security and Medicare to be paid for with offsetting revenue increases or entitlement cuts—not only in the current budget but also over both five- and ten-year spans into the future. If Congress failed to enact those offsets, the law required across-the-board reductions in entitlement programs to prevent an increase in the deficit. Fiscal conservatives and liberals alike credit PAYGO and the discipline it imposed for helping to turn federal deficits into surpluses by the end of the nineties. They attribute much of the enormous increase in the deficit in the past decade to the demise of the PAYGO statute, which expired in 2002.[29]

A pay-as-you-go law could operate the same way in California that it did in Congress in the nineties. The legislature (and the voters at the ballot box, as we'll see in Chapter 9) would require itself to live in the real world of budget trade-offs. Every time it made a change in law with ongoing budget consequences—imposing longer sentences for crimes, creating tax credits, or increasing eligibility, benefits, or provider payments for entitlement programs like Medi-Cal—lawmakers would have to find a way to pay for it over five and ten years with an offsetting policy change. And because some changes have the potential to be fiscally destabilizing over even longer terms, lawmakers would put an automatic ten-year sunset provision on any policy decision subject to PAYGO, so that future legislatures have to revisit it in the light of changed circumstances.

There's no guarantee that PAYGO, had it been in effect in California in 1999, would have headed off the big pension increase, now widely seen as an unsustainable burden on the state budget. Maybe even the Legislative Analyst's Office, which would act as PAYGO's independent umpire, would have bought into the stock bubble mentality. But the odds are good that the pension hike would have been scored as a budget hit, requiring a trade-off. That might not have stopped the speeding train, but it would have prompted the pension debate that California never had.

THROWING AWAY
THE WHIPS AND CHAINS

As important as these three big reforms are to restoring fiscal responsibility in California, they don't belong in California's constitution. And neither do the other whips and chains that now litter it.

Constitutions are not policy documents. They set the relationship between individuals and their government and make the rules by which democracy is played. Democracy's direction is meant to be decided on the field, by voters and their elected leaders, not predetermined by constitutional rules.

In California's constitution, as we have seen, that distinction between framework and policy is hopelessly muddled. The habit of loading the constitution with budget rules, with tax and spending limitations, with spending mandates and protected programs, is deeply ingrained in Californians. This suits the needs of ideological and special-interest groups, which like to be able to turn a one-time majority into a permanent policy choice locked away where it is hard and expensive for others to change it. Other states are offenders in this regard. But California is among the very worst, and worse off for it.

There are better ways. You need look no further than the U.S. Constitution. If you blink, you can miss its few scant provisions dealing with public finance. It contains no fancy mandates, no straitjackets, just a few simple rules establishing the roles of the executive and legislative branches in raising and spending money. Operating within that spare framework, presidents and Congresses have managed for two centuries to make and change fiscal policy in accordance with the voters' wishes. The states that typically earn the highest marks for good management—among them Virginia, Indiana, Iowa, and Minnesota—have no supermajority rules for taxing and spending; they have few, if any, constitutional rules hemming in their budget choices; and they usually have only constitutional provisions for limiting debt, a proper thing to include in a state's fundamental charter so that one generation can't send its bills to those yet unborn or too young to vote. The best-governed states set their fiscal direction by statute and democratic political choice.[30]

California could too. The constitutional fiscal reform that California needs involves mostly subtraction, not addition. Take away supermajority vote requirements for budgets and tax or fee increases. Take away Prop 98. And no more embedding policy choices, whether property tax rates or the apportionment of highway user fees, into the state's fundamental charter; let them be relegated to statute where they belong. When it comes to fiscal provisions in the constitution, let California's motto be: Get them out, get them all out. After years of gridlock and debt, California needs to give democratic budgeting a try.

But here's the catch. Many Californians understand that the state's fiscal system is broken. A lot of them would be prepared, in principle at least, to move to the more democratic budgeting system. But they just don't trust state government, especially the legislature. They are suspicious of an election system dominated by money and the spin that money buys. They believe lawmakers are more often interested in their own careers and the groups that fund them than in the welfare of ordinary people like them. They don't think the legislature, with its many uncompetitive election contests, is responsive to their concerns or can be held accountable for its actions. Moderates believe the legislature is dominated by ideologues of the right and left. Conservatives say it's controlled by public employee unions and dances to the tune of their campaign contributions. Liberals complain it's too beholden to big corporations and special-interest cash. And given California's recent history, you can hardly blame them for thinking those things.

So the path to more responsible and democratic budgeting traverses more strenuous and treacherous terrain than the liberal conventional wisdom imagines. It's not simply a matter of repealing the supermajority vote rules on budgets and taxes.

To begin with, there's the practical political reality: polling suggests that if California voters are to be persuaded to eliminate the two-thirds rules and Prop 98, which they regard (mistakenly) as a way to fiscal

responsibility and quality education, and if they are to give elected officials more fiscal flexibility and discretion, they must be assured that the
people they elect represent their views and can be held accountable if the
legislature puts special interests ahead of the public good.

And then there's what you might call the actual reality. If California
is to have a more democratic system of budgeting, it needs to have a
political and governing system that is more democratic—one that allows
"politically equal citizens to govern themselves under laws and government policies that have been adopted and are maintained with their
rational consent," as political scientist Robert Dahl puts it, where every
citizen's vote counts equally, both in who gets elected and what policies
the legislature enacts.[31]

In other words, real budget reform and political reform are two halves
of the same walnut. California is unlikely to get one without the other.

6

THE ARCHITECTURE
OF POLITICAL FRUSTRATION

The old-timers in California politics remember a better day in Sacramento. "We were there to govern," writes William T. Bagley, a Republican
who represented Marin County in the Assembly from 1961 to 1974.
"Trust and longtime friendships trumped the relatively few ideologues
and, thus, provided the legislative glue. There were no partisan aisles
in the chamber. We sat together, ate together, and played together," he
remembers, the word "play" being his euphemism for what were often
more alcoholic and libidinous pursuits. "What has happened to mod-
eration and compromise?" he asks. They are fallen, he answers, before
the political reform rules that prevent lawmakers from drinking and
whoring together on the lobbyists' dime; the invasion of the legislature
by the post–Prop 13 "Cavemen" conservatives who insisted on sitting and
thinking and voting together as partisans; and the advent of term limits.[1]

You don't need to buy into Bagley's nostalgia or particular interpre-
tation to appreciate that his analysis gets one thing right. California's
politics is the product of two factors. On one side of the equation are the
demographics and political attitudes of Californians; on the other, the
electoral rules and institutions by which those attitudes are expressed and
turned into state policy.

The trouble with much of the reform conversation is that it misses how much the underlying political landscape has changed since Bagley first got elected to the legislature and overestimates how much incremental reforms can change it. This is no longer the California of 15 million people who believed a strong and vigorous government could and should serve the common good. There are more than twice as many of us. And over the past four decades we Californians have been busy sorting and clumping ourselves into wholly new political and cultural alignments.

CALIFORNIA SORTED AND CLUMPED

In Bagley's day, ideology and party did not always cohabitate. The Democratic Party of the mid-twentieth century was an uneasy coalition of left and right. The most Democratic part of the state, by registration, was the San Joaquin Valley, home to migrants who had brought their evangelical religion, conservative attitudes, and party loyalties with them from the South and who liked New Deal–style government spending on water and transportation projects to build their impoverished economy. These rural Democrats were uneasily allied with union workers, Catholics, Jews, and liberals on the coast, and with the African Americans who had also exited Dixie to find jobs and a better way of life away from Jim Crow. The GOP coalition still had its base in Los Angeles, which at the end of World War II had been the whitest Protestant city in the nation—Iowa come to the beach. The Republican Party brought together the traditionally conservative, antilabor forces long championed by the *Los Angeles Times* with more socially liberal probusiness voters in the wealthier suburban coastal areas from Santa Barbara to Marin. In Bagley's California, State Senator Anthony Beilenson, a liberal Jewish Democrat from Beverly Hills, passed the landmark 1967 bill loosening restrictions on abortion with the help of Protestant Republican legislators who believed government didn't belong in the bedroom—over the opposition of Catholic liberal Democrats. The bill was signed into law by Governor Ronald Reagan.[2]

Since then, Californians have swung their partisan identities more in line with their ideological preferences. While the East Coast media joked about "little old ladies in tennis shoes" in California who believed President Dwight Eisenhower was a Communist appeaser and Chief Justice Earl Warren ought to be impeached, those Southern California activists were driving a national movement that would bring all types of conservatives—religious traditionalists alarmed by drugs, sex, abortion, feminism, and crime; whites opposed to racial integration; hawkish anti-communists; libertarian foes of taxes—into the Republican Party, whose reins they would permanently seize with the election of Reagan as president. As these activists made the Republican Party the exclusive home of conservatism, the Democrats increasingly became home to the kinds of Californians who had once fit comfortably in the party of Lincoln and Teddy Roosevelt—civil rights advocates; libertarian foes of mixing religion and politics; environmentalists; supporters of expanded public education; opponents of concentrated wealth and corporate power. Today, you don't need to ask a Californian directly about her partisan identity. If she favors abortion rights, believes poor people have it hard because benefit programs are too stingy, and thinks we are already seeing the effects of global warming, she's most likely a Democrat and almost certainly not a Republican (though her mother and father might once have been).[3]

Even as Californians have been sorting themselves ideologically into Democratic and Republican camps, they have also been gathering geographically into communities of the like-minded. Many of the white Republican-voting families who filled the San Fernando Valley and the new Los Angeles suburbs in the Cold War boom left because their defense industry jobs had disappeared, housing became too expensive, or the neighborhood had too many immigrants. They headed for the Inland Empire, the Central Valley, the Sierra foothills, or one of the new boom cities in Arizona or Nevada, and took their politics with them. Their arrival made those inland areas even less ethnically and racially diverse, and their political energy spurred the conservative Democrats they encountered in their new neighborhoods to make the partisan transition to the Republican Party. The coastal communities they left behind are now filled with immigrants and the children of immigrants, who are more likely to be Latino or Asian, Catholic or non-Christian, and vote as Democrats or like Democrats.

The clumping "is not simply about political partisanship," journalist Bill Bishop writes in *The Big Sort,* his account of how Americans are "tribalizing" themselves. "It is a division in what they value, in how they worship, and in what they expect out of life," a division abetted by the marketing muscle and savvy of consumer products corporations, megachurches, and real estate developers. It is a division that gets reinforced by the echo chamber of living in isolation and consuming media increasingly segmented and targeted to discrete slices of the public.[4]

The word most frequently attached to this phenomenon, "polarization," sounds vaguely scary. It is a favorite of pundits who like to portray themselves as the sensible middle locked in battle with stubborn ideologues on the fringes. But how much concern we attach to it depends a lot on where the poles are planted.

We can take some comfort that the poles where Democrats and Republicans camp out aren't very far apart when measured by the yardstick of our own history (think slavery, Vietnam, or civil rights) or the divisions elsewhere in the democratic world. In this second Gilded Age, Democrats are not so liberal that they did not countenance—or sometimes abet—the vast transfer of income over the past three decades to the richest 1 percent, and the buccaneering in the mortgage and banking industries that eventually led so many to foreclosure, unemployment, and financial ruin in the recent Great Recession. Similarly, today's Republicans are no more conservative than the stand-patters who, except for brief Hiram Johnson and Earl Warren interludes, have held the party's reins since the first Gilded Age in the late nineteenth century. Our tax debates are fierce but the stakes are small—whether taxes will be, by international standards, low or very low. On most of the emotional moral issues, like capital punishment and abortion, one side or the other enjoys a sizable and stable majority in California. As for gay marriage, the social issue that most closely divides the electorate, anyone who looks at the age distribution of yeas and nays on the question knows that our grandchildren will wonder what the fuss was about.

Yet the fact remains that, in a state of nearly 40 million, we are going to have sharp differences. People are going to use politics to pursue their clashing economic interests. People of different religious bents will bring different values and insights to public decisions about sex, love, marriage, and death. Until some great crosscutting issue arises, the two major parties are likely to remain polarized on a liberal-conservative axis. There seems no end in sight to the desire to sort ourselves into neighborhoods where everyone goes to the same church, watches the same cable news shows, trolls the same Web sites, and rarely hears a contrary word.

In other words, the things that most trouble nostalgic reformers like Bagley, the changes that have happened on the political and demographic side of his equation, are here to stay, at least for the immediate future. And because these changes are deeply rooted in our ideas and choices, they are not susceptible to cure by small adjustments on the political reform side of his equation.

What we *can* do is reshape our political system. We can design it so that it faithfully reflects those disagreements and accurately weights them in public representation. As political scientist Robert Dahl writes, a well-functioning democracy "provides strong incentives for political leaders to search for the broadest feasible agreement before adopting a law or policy and yet allows the decision to be made, if need be, by majority vote—always, of course, within limits set by the need to preserve fundamental democratic rights."[5] Many Californians understand that the current system doesn't meet those tests, but few understand why: because our discontent is bred in that system's bone.

A SYSTEM FAMILIAR
AND UNDEMOCRATIC

To understand why, consider what most of us take to be an unexceptional political event: on June 6, 2006, Michael Duvall, two-time mayor of Yorba

Linda, won the Republican primary election in Assembly District 72. The district, Richard Nixon's birthplace and home to his presidential library, is the kind of Orange County bastion the Republican nominee can count on winning in the general election as long as he's breathing. So Duvall's primary victory—with 19,447 votes, a mere 10 percent of the district's registered voters and about 4 percent of the residents in the district—effectively earned him a ticket to Sacramento. With this one victory, he would have likely represented AD 72 for six years to come—that is, had he not, on a July afternoon in 2009, sitting on the Appropriations Committee dais before a microphone he did not know to be live, boasted to a colleague in vivid detail about regularly having that ticket punched by two younger women not his wife (one of them, according to news reports she later denied, a lobbyist paid to influence the committee Duvall co-chaired).

Duvall's legislative technique (or at least the public recital of it) may be uncommon, but his diminutive electoral victory is not. Of the twenty-eight new Assembly members elected in 2008, fifteen of them, like Duvall before them, owed their election to having won the primary votes of 10 percent or fewer of registered voters in a district that is not competitive in the general election.[6] Democratic Assemblyman John A. Pérez from downtown Los Angeles was the most economical. He won only 4,905 votes in his primary, about 5 percent of registered voters or 1 percent of the district's population. With that handful of votes, and the support of his Democratic colleagues, in early 2010 he was elected the speaker of the Assembly, a body that represents 38 million people. The 2008 election was no anomaly. When the other members of the 2009–10 Assembly were first elected, whether in 2004 or 2006, many of them also owed their seats to a similarly tiny share of the electorate in their districts.

The news media rarely find anything odd in this result, and most Californians are unaware of it. It is the system we know. It is the system used in most legislative and congressional races around the country. But if we put familiarity aside for a moment and look at what's actually happening, we see something quite remarkable: our political system routinely allows fewer than 10 percent of the electorate to elect more than half of the lawmakers who make the laws for all of us.

Consider what would happen were some political group or official to propose that we roll back the democratic gains of the past two hundred years, so that only white male property owners, a small slice of the society, elect our representatives. The media would be aghast and voters would bristle. Yet we barely notice that our current political system works to produce a similar outcome. It lets a very small, and often unrepresentative, fraction of the electorate determine who serves in the legislature. Measured against the standard of democracy set in much of the rest of the modern world, our system looks both strange and undemocratic. When it comes to political systems and the machinery of democratic consent, California, home to Google and the iPhone, is still living in the world of the telegraph and stagecoach.

THE ARCHITECTURE OF POLITICAL FRUSTRATION

California's old-fangled electoral system is built of four pieces: winner-take-all elections; plurality victory; single-member geographic districts; and party primaries. Each piece contributes, individually and in combination, in ways we rarely notice, to the political disenchantment that afflicts the state.

Winner-take-all. Every state election contest in California is a zero-sum game. The candidate with the most votes wins the job, and the loser and those who voted for him or her get nothing. This is unavoidable when choosing a governor or another executive post. But it creates an issue when winner-take-all is applied in elections to the legislature, especially in combination with a second feature of California elections, plurality victory.

Plurality victory. Under this rule, also known as "first past the post," a candidate needs to get only one more vote than any other candidate to win an election. California applies this rule to all elections for state office (with the exception of special elections for vacant seats in the legislature, in which case there is a runoff between the leading Republican and the leading Democrat).

In elections with only two candidates, the winner always receives a majority of the votes cast, of course. But in elections with multiple candidates, one can get elected with only a small percentage of the vote—as when you ran against six others for class president in fourth grade and prevailed on the strength of your own vote, the vote of your best buddy, and those of the three classmates to whom you agreed to hand over your lunch money that week. The low vote totals that propel many candidates like Michael Duvall and John Pérez to the legislature are the result of a primary election victory in a field of three or more candidates. But there are often plurality winners in general elections as well. Among the Assembly newcomers in 2009 was Alyson L. Huber, a Democrat representing suburban Sacramento, who was elected despite having a majority of the district vote against her; she won only 46.7 percent of the vote in the general election. The last three governors won with only a plurality in one of their gubernatorial victories—Wilson in 1990, Davis in 2002, and Schwarzenegger in 2003.

Handing victories to candidates who win only a plurality of the vote is the best-understood defect in our system. Americans became all too well acquainted with it in the 2000 presidential election. They saw the rifts that can pull the country apart when a candidate wins with less than a majority of votes—a dissatisfaction amplified in the case of George W. Bush by the operation of the Electoral College, which allowed him to ascend to the White House without even a plurality. They learned from the Florida debacle about how plurality elections permitted "spoilers" like Ralph Nader to produce an election outcome that ran contrary to the wishes of a majority of that state's voters. Long before Florida, in a 1984 Sacramento-area State Senate campaign, California had encountered plurality elections and spoilers in an even more malign form. Veteran independent senator Ray Johnson was defeated by Republican John Doolittle when Doolittle secretly funded a token Democratic candidate as a spoiler to siphon votes away from Johnson.[7] At its best, the rule of plurality victory elects candidates who are more unwanted than wanted; at its worst, it permits cynical manipulation of elections.

Single-member geographic districts. California apportions the membership of the legislature in geographic districts, eighty for the Assembly and forty for the Senate, each of which is represented by a single member who won the most votes in the previous election. This system, when combined with winner-take-all plurality elections, is known in the political science trade as single-member plurality elections. It has predictable side effects, many of them quite unpleasant for anyone who cares about the health of California's democracy.

The most obvious of these is that on election day the votes of millions of Californians are totally irrelevant. If you support the winning candidate for an Assembly or State Senate seat, you end up with a representative who comes close to reflecting your values and priorities. You are more likely to feel comfortable approaching the legislator you helped elect, and that legislator is more likely to attend to your needs and those of the other voters and groups who joined you in electing her. But if you voted for one of the losing candidates, you might as well not have shown up at the polls; you don't have a voice in the legislature. Except in (the relatively rare) cases where the district is politically competitive, your legislator has little or no political incentive to spend time and energy addressing your concerns. You don't count. And you may never count: as we'll see, millions of Californians live in legislative districts where they are likely to remain in perpetual political minority status.

"It is an essential part of democracy that minorities should be adequately represented," John Stuart Mill, the great theorist of liberty, wrote in his treatise on democratic representation. "No real democracy, nothing but a false show of democracy, is possible without it." By this standard, California democracy doesn't measure up.[8]

It is hard to say which minorities should feel most aggrieved by the effects of this system. There are, for example, the Californians who belong to one of the minor parties, or who consider themselves independents. One of the iron laws of political science is that single-member plurality districts cement a two-party system in government.[9] As a practical matter, the high hurdle of winning a plurality in a district makes it difficult for third or fourth parties to gain representation in the legislature. Only when third parties can muster a strong appeal concentrated in particular geographic areas are they likely to win elections. That difficulty is compounded by voter psychology. Voters fear that supporting a minor party whose platform they may prefer will waste their votes and perhaps help the party they like least by creating a spoiler effect.

All this might not be worth worrying about if Californians were happy with the choices offered by the two major parties. But they are not. "Decline to state" voters, those who give no party preference when they register to vote, are the fastest-growing segment of the California electorate. They made up 19.5 percent of the total for the 2008 general election. In a poll leading up to that vote, 52 percent of Californians said they believe a third major political party is needed because the two major parties are not doing an adequate job of governing.[10] The current electoral system stands in the way of a development half the electorate would welcome.

But you can also make the case that Republicans should feel most slighted. Single-member plurality districts, by their nature, exaggerate the strength of the majority party.

To understand why, imagine if good-government reformers of the Common Cause kind woke up to their perfect political world: a California in which voters are randomly distributed by party preference and every legislative district is fairly drawn, so that each district exactly matches the partisan makeup of the state as a whole. If voters followed their party registration preferences, with independents splitting their votes between the major parties, Democrats would get about 54 percent of the vote— and win every seat!

In the real world, the majority party in California, the Democrats, gets a small but real boost in representation from the current system. In the 2008 Assembly elections, Democrats won fifty-one seats (63.8 percent of the total) despite having received just 57.8 percent of the votes—five more seats than they would have won if the seats had been awarded in proportion to the number of votes the party's candidates had received.

Finally, there's the question that has dominated political debate in California over the past three decades: who should draw the lines? In the power to draw legislative districts rests the power to decide elections. Complaints about the political abuse of that power are as old as the Republic; the term for that abuse, gerrymandering, hallows the cartographic skills of Elbridge Gerry, governor of Massachusetts in 1812. Most people agree that, in principle, districts ought to be "fair," with voters picking their representatives and not the other way round. Beyond agreement on lofty principle, there is only hand-to-hand partisan combat. Many Californians, especially Republicans, disliked U.S. Representative Phillip Burton's notorious 1982 House redistricting plan for California, a gerrymander in which he protected some of his Democratic friends ("You're in your mother's arms," Burton would tell them as he worked his plan)[11] and punished a couple of his conservative enemies. Hardly anyone but Democratic politicians noticed that the plan produced the next decade by the Republican-dominated California Supreme Court was even more tilted toward the GOP than Burton's plan had been toward Democrats.

By general agreement, the bipartisan plan adopted by the legislature during the next redistricting in 2001 was "fair" in that it had no partisan tilt toward either party. Seats held by Democrats were made safer for Democrats; those held by Republicans were made safer for Republicans. The plan also left almost no competitive seats. That arrangement pleased the parties but angered Californians naive enough to believe that the outcomes of elections ought not to be decided before voters go to the polls.[12]

Party primaries. The political parties are not free, as they once were in the nineteenth century, to choose the nominees they offer to voters on the general election ballot for state office. Big Government took on the role of regulating party nominations in 1909 with the passage of a direct primary law, a Progressive reform. Under a direct primary system, party nominees are elected by voters registered in that party and (if the party permits) independent voters who choose to vote in that party's primary. Primary elections typically attract only the most active and informed base voters in each party. As we saw above, primaries are often won, with relatively small pluralities, by the candidate who most successfully energizes party loyalists and raises the most money from the special interest groups that lobby at the state capitol.

The Progressive idea behind the direct party primary was to take the nominating process out of the hands of party activists ("bosses") and their allied interests groups (the railroad and trusts) and hand it to the people. A century later, today's reformers rail against the very system that the Progressives created—and make the very same complaint: that the current system is dominated by party activists ("wingnuts" and "moonbeams") and their allied interest groups (big business, Indian gaming tribes, public employee unions). Political reform is what we do in California to break our hearts.

Each of these pieces of the current system, examined in isolation, delivers results that are less than wholly democratic. Taken together, they amplify the effects of partisan polarization and the geographic clumping of the like-minded. They yield a legislature of mostly liberals and conservatives to represent a state where many voters consider themselves to be moderates or would like to vote for a third party. They ensure that Republicans living in the Bay Area and Democrats living in the Sierra foothills (and Greens and Libertarians living anywhere) will never be represented in the legislature. They make it unlikely that legislators will ever have a political incentive to step out of partisan mode to craft policies that command a consensus in the state. Is it any wonder that Californians are so unhappy with the representation they receive in Sacramento?

THE HEARTBREAK OF
REDISTRICTING REFORM

California voters took a first step toward changing this system in November 2008, when they narrowly approved Proposition 11, a measure supported by Governor Schwarzenegger and reform groups like Common Cause. It created a Citizens Redistricting Commission to take over the task of drawing new Assembly, Senate, and Board of Equalization (but not congressional) districts after each federal census, beginning in 2011.

"Citizens Redistricting Commission" is something of a misnomer. No one who in the previous ten years has done what active citizens do—work on or for a political campaign or party; serve in an appointed office; work as a staff member for, or a consultant to, a public official; run for office; lobby any level of government; make a political contribution of $2,000 to a candidate; even switch their party registration to vote in the party primary election they regard as most important—may serve on the commission. Nor may any person who is closely related, by blood or marriage, to such a dangerously civic-minded citizen. The next set of district lines will be drawn by fourteen political virgins who have applied for the job (it pays $300 a day), who have been vetted by a team of auditors for "relevant analytical skills, ability to be impartial, and appreciation for California's diverse demographics and geography," and who have survived blackballing by legislative leaders. There will be no more gerrymanders of California legislative districts—unless the gerrymander is delivered by the commission itself, which is accountable to no one and subject only to the check of a referendum on its proposed maps.

Reformers have attached high hopes to this change. The conventional wisdom in Sacramento holds that the 2001 bipartisan gerrymander, by reducing the number of competitive elections to a minimum, spurred polarization in the state capitol and worsened gridlock. "Gerrymandering tends to reward extremism in both parties and punish compromise, locking lawmakers into ideological corners," George Skelton, state capital columnist for the *Los Angeles Times,* wrote in support of Prop 11.[13] But as a cure for all the things said to ail our politics—polarized parties, lack of political competition, unresponsive representation—redistricting reform is like prescribing aspirin for gangrene.

Contrary to the wisdom of chat shows and op-ed pages, the evidence from political science research shows redistricting to have had little or nothing to do with legislative polarization or declining electoral competition. In a careful study of partisan polarization before and after the 2001 redistricting, Eric McGhee of the Public Policy Institute of California found that, "On every dimension—economic, environmental, social, and overall party loyalty—there is little evidence that the 2001 redistricting had an effect on the partisanship of the Legislature." His conclusion? "If bridging the partisan divide in Sacramento is the paramount objective, redistricting reform would be a poor way to achieve it."[14]

If it's more competition we want, redistricting reform is also likely to prove weak medicine. "There is no evidence that redistricting by nonpartisan redistricting commissions or courts resulted in more competitive districts than redistricting by partisan state legislatures," Emory University political scientists found in a 2006 study of declining competition in U.S. House of Representatives elections. Incumbents' money advantage and voter self-sorting were more important factors.[15] That should come as little surprise to Californians, who learned the limits of nonpartisan redistricting in the 1990s. The state went through five legislative election cycles using districts drawn in 1991 by the state supreme court. Even under maps ostensibly drawn with no attention to protecting incumbents, only 5 percent of California House and Assembly elections ended in a party turnover. That's a bit more competition than under the current districts. But it wasn't enough to make Californians feel good about government or the quality of representation they received.

Prop 11 is unlikely to yield a different result. The partisan makeup of geographic districts flows from two very different kinds of decisions: those of the mapmakers about where to draw lines, and those of millions of Californians about where to live. In today's California (and in the rest of the country too) our decisions about where to live are by far the more powerful force.

"Redistricting is limited in its capacity to create a heavily competitive state," wrote Bruce E. Cain, California's leading scholar of redistricting, in a 2008 study. California's new political geography, with Democrats controlling the coast and Republicans dominating inland areas, affords few chances to draw competitive districts. There are no Republican seats to be conjured up in the Bay Area, no Democratic seats to be summoned in the Sierra or northern Sacramento Valley. It would take the most brazen gerrymander, slithering across the landscape in the name of competition and ignoring all constitutional and good government rules, to make even half of the legislative seats competitive, Cain has found.[16]

The new independent redistricting commission does not even have that option. The law tells it to draw districts that are contiguous and compact and minimize the splitting of cities, counties, and communities of interest. Forget for a minute that those criteria are often mutually exclusive. Cities and counties themselves often fail the tests of compactness and contiguity; the map of Bakersfield, for example, most closely resembles the residue of a milkshake dropped on the road from a car doing 65 mph on Highway 99. The important thing here is that the law *forbids* the commissioners from considering any possible effects on political parties, candidates, or incumbents. In other words, they cannot even look at the factors that determine electoral competitiveness. The virgins will perform their work wearing political blindfolds. Any increase in electoral competition will likely be small and purely accidental. Prop 11 has the heartbreak already built in.

TILTING THE PLAYING FIELD WITH PRIMARY REFORM

Redistricting reform is aimed at restoring fairness to California elections. Primary election reform, in contrast, has been a political effort by one team to reshape the electoral playing field to make it easier for its own candidates to win more games.

The rightward realignment of the California Republican Party has created a peculiar political problem for the corporate titans of the new California information economy. The kind of candidates they like to support—attentive to the interests of business and the wealthy, but also socially liberal and interested in education, infrastructure, and the environment—are about as welcome to Republican Party primary voters as a labor union organizer at a Los Altos Hills wine-tasting party.

Tom Campbell has long been the poster boy for their problem. The son of a prominent Democratic federal judge in Chicago, Campbell became that rarest of creatures, an intellectual in politics, by way of a Harvard law degree and a doctorate in economics earned at the University of Chicago under the tutelage of conservative economist Milton Friedman. After stints in the Reagan administration and as a professor at Stanford University Law School, he was elected to the U.S. House of Representatives in 1988 to occupy the Mid-Peninsula Bay Area seat held for many years by maverick Republican Pete McCloskey. A social liberal and a free-market champion, Campbell was the very model of a modern moderate, the kind of candidate who quickened the hearts of editorial writers, opened the wallets of Silicon Valley donors, and—his supporters claimed—most closely reflected the views of California's voters. But across his path to advancement in California politics lay a roadblock closely guarded by the conservative voters in a statewide Republican primary. They had little use for candidates like Campbell with their unsound views on abortions, gays, guns, and the environment. The big-business establishment cleared the 1990 GOP gubernatorial primary for one of its favorites, Pete Wilson, but could not do the same for Campbell, who lost the 1992 U.S. Senate primary to conservative radio talk-show host Bruce Herschensohn.

Unable to prevail at the ballot box, Campbell and his allies set out to change the rules of the game. With funding from Silicon Valley grandees like David Packard, a co-founder of Hewlett-Packard, they qualified and passed a 1996 initiative, Proposition 198, to create what political scientists call a "blanket primary." The idea was to get their favorites through Republican primaries by opening up those contests to outside voters—either independents or visiting Democrats. The hope was that such candidates, once nominated, would prove more appealing to the statewide electorate than the red-meat conservatives normally selected in Republican-only primaries.

When voters took the blanket primary for a test drive in June 1998, it performed, in some ways, as advertised. Under the new primary, all voters got a ballot listing all of the primary contestants in every party. They were permitted to march down the ballot, merrily switching from party to party as they moved from one office to the next. They could vote in the Republican primary for the U.S. Senate, then dabble in the Democratic primary for governor, and finally return to the GOP fold to choose that party's Assembly nominee. And millions of Californians did just that. More than one-fifth of Democrats and nearly one-quarter of Republicans crossed over into at least one of the other party's contests. They were especially likely to cross over if they belonged to the minority party in safe districts, where the winners of the majority party's primary would almost certainly head off to Sacramento or Washington after being rubber-stamped in the November general election. In several such districts around the state, crossover Democratic and independent voters propelled moderate Republicans to victory in contests against hard-line social conservatives. Charlene Zettel won the Republican primary in the 75th Assembly District even though she received fewer votes from Republicans than from crossover Democrats.[17]

Results like that pleased the blanket primary's supporters but proved its constitutional undoing. The political parties sued to invalidate the reform on the ground that government was taking from them their constitutional right under the First Amendment to have their own members pick their own nominees. The U.S. Supreme Court agreed. "Proposition 198 forces political parties to associate with—to have their nominees, and hence their positions, determined by—those who, at best, have refused to affiliate with the party, and, at worst, have expressly affiliated with a rival," Justice Antonin Scalia wrote for a seven-member majority of the court in 2000. "Such forced association has the likely outcome—indeed, in this case the *intended* outcome—of changing the parties' message. We can think of no heavier burden on a political party's associational freedom" (italics in original).[18]

As a fallback, those wanting to remake the electoral rules to their political advantage have seized on a second primary reform, known as the "jungle" or "top two" primary. Voters turned it down in 2004 when it was put on the ballot as Proposition 62, a measure funded again with $5 million from big business and Silicon Valley (this time with Countrywide Financial, the mortgage lender that would soon crater and be taken over by Bank of America, as the largest donor). But the legislature put the jungle primary on the ballot again in 2010 as part of the payoff to Republican state senator Abel Maldonado for his budget vote in the February 2009 crisis.

The jungle primary effectively ends party nominations for office in California. All candidates appear on the same ballot, where each can list a party "preference" or not. As in the blanket primary, any voter, without regard to party registration, can vote for any candidate for an office. But there is a critical difference. In the blanket primary the candidate receiving the most votes in each party advances to the November general election ballot. In the jungle primary only the top two vote-getters for each office—even if they are both from the same party—are "nominated" to run against each other in the general election. When the state of Washington first used a jungle primary in 2008, most primary contests ended with a Republican and a Democrat advancing to the general election. But in 7 of 124 legislative contests, voters selected two candidates of the same party to compete in November.[19]

As an instrument to elect more "moderate" Republicans to the legislature, the jungle primary is an inferior substitute for the blanket primary. In 1998, Democrats who lived in Republican-leaning districts could strategically hedge in the primary without fear. They could cross over to vote in the GOP contest to help a second-choice candidate, the less conservative Republican, win the primary. But they helped the Republicans pick a candidate safe in the knowledge that they could vote for their top choice, the Democratic nominee, in the general election. Political scientist Thad Kousser found that nearly half of the crossover voters, after having cast a risk-free hedge vote in the primary, returned home to support their own party's nominee in the general election.

A jungle primary, however, makes hedge voting dicier. Because only the two candidates with the most votes advance, voters cannot count on their top-choice candidates appearing on the November ballot unless they vote for them in the primary. They will be reluctant to take the chance except in elections in which they believe there is no possibility that their own party can advance a candidate to the general election. The great irony here is that the jungle primary will make a difference in legislative races only to the extent that the new independent redistricting reform draws lots of safe and uncompetitive districts.

But for any small gains in advancing the kinds of candidates favored by big business, there will be costs to our politics and freedoms. A jungle primary, like the blanket primary and California's old cross-filing system, helps incumbents—an odd thing to do at a time when incumbents have so many other advantages, including campaign dollars. It gives general election voters fewer choices; sometimes they will have only one major party to choose from, and almost all the time they will see no third-party or independent candidate on their ballots. It will impose on millions of Democratic and Republican primary voters who live in safe districts the same dilemma third-party voters now face in most general elections: whether to vote for the candidate who best represents their preferences and thereby give up all influence on who represents their district, or for a second-best choice to head off victory by a candidate they despise. There are a lot of adjectives you can apply to a mechanism that requires so many citizens to skip over their first choices and cast votes while holding their noses. But "democratic" is not among them.

The jungle primary also tramples on the First Amendment rights of political parties in the same way the blanket primary did. The U.S. Supreme Court in 2008 rejected an invitation to find the Washington jungle primary unconstitutional before it had been put to use and demonstrated any harm. But as Justice Scalia noted in dissent, there is no public interest behind a jungle primary other than the Washington state government's "dislike for bright-colors partisanship, and its desire to blunt the ability of political parties with noncentrist views to endorse and advocate their own candidates." The corporate captains who have promoted the jungle primary would no doubt object if government were to declare that any person is free to declare himself Apple or Google and sell products under their brand names. But the jungle primary allows "any candidate to use the ballot for drawing upon the goodwill that a party has developed, while preventing the party from using the ballot to reject the claimed association or to identify the genuine candidate of its choice," Scalia wrote. A conservative Supreme Court is unlikely to let Big Government force counterfeit candidates on the parties for long.[20]

The heartbreak of primary reform in California is that it is unnecessary to infringe on the First Amendment rights of political parties to have fair and representative elections. There are better options:

Open primary. Used in twenty-seven states, an open primary permits voters, either publicly or privately, to choose on election day in which party's primary they would like to participate. Unlike the blanket primary, in which voters can skip back and forth between parties on a single ballot, the open primary poses no constitutional issue. Because the voters in an open primary chose to affiliate with one party, and that party alone, for that election, the Supreme Court has ruled that the open primary does not violate the First Amendment protection of free association. Unlike the jungle primary, an open primary does not limit voter choice in the general election, does not harm third parties, and does not force many voters to cast votes for their second-choice candidate.

Semiclosed primary. In this system, as in the primary system California used for most elections in recent decades, each party's primary is open to its own registered voters and to independents who wish to vote in it. There is one critical difference: voters are permitted to register on election day, making it possible for them to choose the primary in which they wish to participate—not weeks or months in advance, but when it matters, at the polls, after the campaigns have been conducted and voters have more information upon which to base their choice. Political scientists have found that elections in states with open and semiclosed primaries yield winners closest to the views of voters in their district, which is exactly what primary reformers in California say they want.[21]

In the end, though, the political reform agenda shouldn't be about rejiggering the rules of politics to advance one particular point of view. The better and more democratic choice is to get rid of primary elections altogether. How does California do that? By finally taking seriously a principle embedded near the beginning of the state's constitution: "A voter who casts a vote in an election in accordance with the laws of this State shall have that vote counted."[22]

Narrowly read, that provision means that every ballot legally cast should be added to the election tally. Read as a statement of democratic principle, it means something more: that every vote should be equally meaningful in electing those who represent us in the state capitol and elsewhere. This reading is no stretch. It is exactly why we Californians find gerrymandering so dismaying. When districts are drawn to determine the outcomes of elections before anyone votes, gerrymandering renders millions of votes meaningless. It is at the root of our dismay when, through the combination of geographic districts and primary elections, so few votes can determine so many of our representatives in Sacramento. Californians don't just believe every vote should be counted; they believe every vote should count. Fortunately for the state, there are proven ways to move beyond its outmoded system and do just that.[23]

7

REMAKING ELECTIONS
AND THE LEGISLATURE

In much of the rest of the democratic world, and particularly outside the former British colonies, nations have rejected single-member plurality electoral systems in favor of proportional representation to elect their legislative bodies.[1] They have found that proportional representation (PR) "is better at ensuring that the maximum number of citizens are represented, that both majorities and minorities have a say in government, that all parties have their fair share of seats in legislatures, that seats change in response to changes in voter views, that the majority rules, and that policymakers faithfully reflect the political views of the majority of the electorate," as political scientist Douglas Amy aptly put it.[2] That summary, of course, reads exactly like the wish list of every California reformer and every Californian who wants the legislature to be more representative, more accountable, and more deliberative.

Before we explore some ways California might use PR to revamp how it elects the legislature, let's first understand how it differs from the current system.

Today, voters whose favored legislative candidate receives one more vote than any other get their views represented in Sacramento; those on the losing side, even if they make up a majority of the district, get no representation at all. In contrast, voters in a PR system receive representation for their views roughly in proportion to their numbers in the electorate.

Today, voters elect legislators from single-member districts, in which geography often predetermines the outcome, either through a deliberate act of gerrymandering or by the action of the demographic invisible hand that has been sorting Californians into communities of the like-minded. Under PR, voters elect legislators from multimember districts, with the seats distributed among parties according to the share of the vote they win. The shape of the districts has little or no influence on the makeup of the legislative body.

Today, the electoral system pushes California into a two-party straitjacket. It exaggerates the strength of the majority party, emphasizes the views of each party's most partisan voters, and closes out independent and minor-party voices. Under PR, the emphasis is on full and accurate representation of voices across the political spectrum and on building coalitions and consensus among them.

As an alternative, proportional representation offers many different models to draw on, though again it offers no single or perfect way to elect a legislature. Each state or nation has different demographic and cultural circumstances. And, of course, there is no virgin birth in electoral design; every system gets its DNA through the sweaty grapplings and exertions of politics, so that few systems look exactly alike. But to understand how PR could improve representation and make every Californian's vote count, let's briefly walk through two models that California might try on for size and fit.

MULTIMEMBER DISTRICTS WITH PROPORTIONAL REPRESENTATION

The first alternative would be to junk the current system of single-member plurality districts in favor of the most common electoral system in the world, and the one with the longest pedigree in the United States: electing legislators from multimember districts using proportional representation. Instead of picking one representative in each of eighty Assembly and forty Senate districts, California would elect five legislators each in sixteen Assembly districts and eight Senate districts, using a voting system that would determine the winners in proportion to the percentage of the vote they received.[3]

It's easy to see how this would change California's politics. Any candidate or party able to command at least 20 percent of the vote in a five-member district would win one of the seats. In other words, even with the sorting of California into Democratic blocs on the coast and Republican blocs inland, there would be no more uncompetitive districts, no more uncontested elections. Republicans in the Bay Area would compete and win seats, and Democratic voters in the Central Valley and Sierra foothills could elect one or more of their own to the legislature. Most districts would be divided three to two between the parties, with the very real possibility that seats could switch between them. Majority control of the legislature would potentially be on the line in every election, and every vote in every part of the state would matter in determining the outcome.

There are a lot of dials to turn and sliders to adjust in designing a legislative electoral system with multimember districts. The number of members elected from a district determines how friendly it will be to minor parties and to a range of opinions in the legislature. Having fewer members per district favors the two major parties and reduces the probability that they will lose or gain seats in an election. Having more members per district lowers the threshold for the number of votes it would take to elect a Green or a Libertarian, and also makes it easier for smaller ethnic or religious groups to elect one of their own. Also, it's not necessary for every district to be the same size or elect the same number of legislators. As long as the districts have equal populations per legislator elected—thus meeting the constitutional requirements of equal representation—California could size and shape the districts to fit the state's distinct regions and their associated media markets, thereby spurring attention to regional needs. The sparsely populated northern third of the state could have a three-member district while the urban areas could have districts of six to eight members.

Beyond the issue of how many members should be chosen in each district, there is the question of how they should be elected. In most systems using multimember districts, each party offers voters a list of candidates in each district. Voters select the party list they prefer, with seats being awarded according to the proportion of votes each party list receives. If this system were applied to our hypothetical five-member legislative districts, voters would get a ballot listing the five candidates offered by each party (see Figure 2). Independent candidates could also appear on the ballot. Voters would cast a vote for the party list they prefer. Let's assume that Democrats get roughly 44 percent of the vote, Republicans get 40 percent, and the Green Party gets 16 percent. The result? Under the proportional representation formula commonly used in such elections, the top two candidates on the Democratic list, the top two candidates on the Republican list, and the top Green candidate would head off to Sacramento.[4]

Many people might want to reject this idea out of hand because they feel uncomfortable voting for a party list instead of directly for a candidate. It's just not something Americans do, they would argue. That premise is debatable. After all, in the most important election we Americans vote in, for president, we are actually choosing party electors of the Electoral College. Moreover, in California's legislative contests, most of which are conducted with little or no media coverage, voters are typically making their choices based on the party label of the candidate, not any informed understanding of the candidate's personal views or character. We Californians may say we hate political parties, but most of us are party animals.

However, it's not necessary to have this argument. California can have multimember districts with proportional representation and still allow voters to choose among candidates. Instead of offering voters only the choice of party lists, the ballot could allow voters in a five-member district to cast votes for any of the candidates on those lists, without regard to party (see Figure 3). In the tally, each vote would count as both a vote for

OFFICIAL BALLOT
Election for the California Assembly
District Twelve
(Five seats to be filled)

Voting Instructions
1. Fill in the circle UNDER the party for which you want to vote.
2. Fill in only ONE circle.

DEMOCRATIC	GREEN	LIBERTARIAN	REPUBLICAN	INDEPENDENT
○	○	○	○	○
1. Juan Flores	1. Jo Shore	1. Chuck Smith	1. Jack Napoli	1. Ben Wilde
2. Maria Polsby	2. Ellen Yee	2. Lance Stewart	2. Pete Jones	
3. James Kim	3. Mike Murray	3. Trudy Rand	3. Mary Alvarez	
4. Olivia Gomez	4. José Salazar	4. Bill Crane	4. Chester Adams	
5. Leif Newsom	5. Claire Silver	5. Peter Drew	5. Sally Williams	

Figure 2   Sample Ballot for Multimember Legislative Districts: Party List

the candidate and a vote for her party. The party votes would determine the division of seats among the parties and the candidate votes would determine which candidates in each party occupy those seats in the legislature. In this system, known as an open party list, every vote would do double duty. It would count toward setting the state's agenda and toward picking the individual lawmakers best able to turn it into action.[5]

Adopting both multimember districts and proportional representation elections would transform legislative politics. To begin with, there

OFFICIAL BALLOT
Election for the California Assembly
District Twelve
(Five seats to be filled)

Voting Instructions
1. Fill in the circle UNDER the candidate for whom you wish to vote.
2. Fill in only ONE circle.
3. Your vote counts for both your candidate and your party.

DEMOCRATIC	GREEN	LIBERTARIAN	REPUBLICAN	INDEPENDENT
1. Juan Flores ◯	1. Jo Shore ◯	1. Chuck Smith ◯	1. Jack Napoli ◯	1. Ben Wilde ◯
2. Maria Polsby ◯	2. Ellen Yee ◯	2. Lance Stewart ◯	2. Pete Jones ◯	
3. James Kim ◯	3. Mike Murray ◯	3. Trudy Rand ◯	3. Mary Alvarez ◯	
4. Olivia Gomez ◯	4. José Salazar ◯	4. Bill Crane ◯	4. Chester Adams ◯	
5. Leif Newsom ◯	5. Claire Silver ◯	5. Peter Drew ◯	5. Sally Williams ◯	

Figure 3   Sample Ballot for Multimember Legislative Districts: Open List

would be real election contests where now there are mostly coronations in safe seats. In PR elections, each party has good reason to run a hard campaign and strong candidates in every district, since each vote it adds to its column, either by attracting new voters to the process or by luring voters away from the other parties, increases its chances of winning an extra seat. Because even small swings in voter preferences could change the distribution of seats in a district, both major parties would be forced to address the concerns of voters they now ignore. Los Angeles Democrats would have to explain to independent voters why they protect the huge pensions of public workers while slashing school funding and social services; Central Valley Republicans would have to explain to suburban mothers whose kids have asthma why they vote against cleaning up the San Joaquin Valley's dirty air.

Notice that the change here involves not just forcing candidates to pay more attention to the voters. This system also yields a different kind of attention, one more focused on issues than on the qualities of individual candidates. Head-to-head contests in single-member plurality elections discourage candidates from being specific about controversial issues, for fear of alienating swing voters; there's no politician more mumble-mouthed than one running in a competitive district. Head-to-head contests encourage mudslinging and other forms of negative politicking. By contrast, PR elections in multimember districts don't pit candidate against candidate, but agendas against agendas. Parties that try to duck issues important to significant groups of the electorate risk having other parties scoop up their votes. The things that matter to voters—whether they are water, air quality, and low incomes in the Central Valley or traffic congestion and bad schools in Los Angeles—would be at the heart of the election discussion.

Today, such discussions rarely happen in state legislative campaigns. Except in the more rural areas, where a media market might contain only one or two legislative districts, most legislative contests get scant public notice. Urban areas contain so many Assembly and Senate seats that broadcast stations and metropolitan newspapers give their elections little coverage. Devoting airtime or column inches to follow the election in Assembly District 54 may please a few prospective voters in San Pedro, but it invites the viewers in the rest of the vast Los Angeles media market to hit the remote or turn the page. Today, covering legislative elections makes little business sense for commercial media. And because most Californians get their political information from those media, the media's pursuit of economic rationality renders most legislative elections invisible to most voters. As a result, these contests typically play out in obscurity and often degenerate into "gotcha" attacks based on small personal foibles. Voters learn which candidate took how much in legislative per diem payments, but nothing about how the candidates would reduce traffic congestion. This is particularly true for primary election campaigns, where the great majority of legislative seats are effectively won. By contrast, with multimember districts sized to encompass whole media markets or at least large chunks of them, campaigns would be more likely to receive coverage in the commercial news media and use paid advertising in regional media to make their case to voters, increasing the amount of information available to the public.

What stands in the way of reinvigorating California governance and citizenship in this way? Some people argue that multimember districts and proportional representation are too complicated for Americans. They ask us to believe Californians would find it hard to use a system that works well in dozens of countries and was used in Illinois from 1870 to 1980 and in two dozen U.S. cities beginning in the Progressive era. (It was dropped in most of the cities when it proved to work too well, electing African Americans and third-party candidates in places where their presence on city bodies wasn't welcome.)[6] This argument—that Californians are too stupid to vote in truly democratic elections—is based more on advanced self-loathing than evidence.

Another argument points to the history of Italy and Israel to imply that PR systems lead to many minor parties and unstable coalition governments. But the overall record of countries that use proportional representation in creating stable governments is quite good. And, as noted above,

California could design its system to avoid the mistakes made in Italy and Israel, which set very low thresholds for representation and thereby invited the proliferation of small parties in their legislative bodies.

A more cogent argument against moving to multimember districts is that they break the geographic tie between elected representatives and the areas they represent. Given the enormous population of California's current legislative districts, that tie currently isn't very strong. But, if we want to keep single-member districts for their coziness, it isn't necessary to forget about proportional representation. California can have both.

THE BEST OF BOTH WORLDS

The best way of combining our familiar single-member districts with proportional representation is with a system known as "mixed-member." Adopted originally in West Germany after World War II, in large part because of the work of American advisers, mixed-member has now spread more widely, "with the promise of providing the best of both the dominant nineteenth- and twentieth-century worlds of electoral systems," write political scientists Matthew Shugart and Martin Wattenberg.[7]

In a mixed-member system, Californians would cast two votes on election day: one vote for the individual they want to represent their local district, and a second vote for a party list of candidates to fill at-large seats in the legislature. As in the current system, the candidate who wins the most votes in each district would be elected to the legislature. The remaining seats in the legislature would be filled at-large from the ranked party lists submitted to voters. The seats would be awarded to the parties so that the total of their district seats and at-large seats equals the proportion of party votes cast. (For a sample ballot, see Figure 4.) In other words, Californians would retain what is most familiar and friendly about the current system—an individual representative tied to a particular place—while having all the democratic advantages offered by multimember districts and proportional representation. It is an opportunity to have the best of both worlds.

As with a multimember system, there are lots of choices to make

OFFICIAL BALLOT
Election for the California Assembly
San Diego Region
District 71
(Five regional seats and one district seat to be filled)

Voting Instructions

Fill in ONE circle UNDER the party you wish to represent the region.

DEMOCRATIC	GREEN	LIBERTARIAN	REPUBLICAN	INDEPENDENT
◯	◯	◯	◯	◯
1. Juan Flores	1. Jo Shore	1. Chuck Smith	1. Jack Napoli	1. Ben Wilde
2. Maria Polsby	2. Ellen Yee	2. Lance Stewart	2. Pete Jones	
3. James Kim	3. Mike Murray	3. Trudy Rand	3. Mary Alvarez	
4. Olivia Gomez	4. José Salazar	4. Bill Crane	4. Chester Adams	
5. Leif Newsom	5. Claire Silver	5. Peter Drew	5. Sally Williams	

DISTRICT 71 Fill in ONE circle next to the candidate you wish to represent the district.

MIKE RICHARDS	Green	◯
GEORGE G. WALKER	Republican	◯
CAMILLE CALDERON	Democratic	◯
WILLIAM BENTLEY	Libertarian	◯
ALICIA NAVARRO	Independent	◯

Figure 4   Sample Ballot for Multimember Legislative Districts: Mixed-Member Voting

about the design of this kind of best-of-both-worlds arrangement. One is about the size of the at-large district in which party-list candidates run. In some countries, the parties run at large across the whole nation. In others they run in smaller areas, such as states or regions. Because California is so large and has such distinctive regions, each with its own economy and issues, it would be best to conduct the at-large party-list vote region by region, so each region has an election in which the parties must spell out how they propose to deal with its specific problems. Other design choices include how high a vote threshold to set before a party wins a share of seats in Sacramento and what system to use to elect the lawmakers from local districts.[8]

A mixed-member system would be good medicine for California's ailments. Like the multimember system we described in the previous section, it would make every vote and every voter count, curing the faults of the single-member plurality elections. It would improve the nature and tone of campaigns. It would make the parties accountable for their performance at the state capitol—voters could easily toss out the majority party or majority coalition—while improving voters' ability to hold their own representative locally accountable. Because voters would determine the party balance in the legislature through the party-list vote, it would end partisan gerrymandering as a factor in state politics.

And it would be easy for voters to understand: Cast one vote for a neighbor to represent your community, one vote for the party to lead the legislature.

GOING UNICAMERAL

The distance between that legislature and the people it is supposed to represent is not merely a problem of election systems. The size and shape of the body itself must be considered. California has seen plenty of discussion about how to change the body, but most of the chatter has been misdirected, focusing on a return to a part-time legislature. What California really should be talking about is a one-part legislature.

Having a legislative branch with two houses (a bicameral legislature) is, like the state's single-member plurality districts, an eighteenth-century relic inherited from America's English colonial masters. When creating our federal system, the framers of the U.S. Constitution followed the English example with the two-house structure in Congress, creating a House of Representatives to represent the people and an aristocratic Senate to represent the states—the latter the most enduringly undemocratic part of our Constitution.[9] California replicated that model in its own legislative branch. But after the 1962 "one man, one vote" decision of the U.S. Supreme Court, which required state legislative districts to be of equal populations, states could no longer apportion one house of their legislature by geography. Both houses now represent voters, not territory.

Most of the arguments for having two houses are just as outmoded as the ermine-collared robes worn in the British House of Lords. People once thought of the State Senate as the "upper house," a chamber of wise old men serving four-year terms and deliberating more seriously than their "lower house" brethren, their longer tenure supposedly a check on the democratic enthusiasm of the Assembly. Sitting in the Senate was an honor a mere assemblyman longed to attain.

All that has disappeared with term limits. Senators will now duck out of the last two years of a term to grab an open Assembly seat or a place on a county board of supervisors. The distinctions between the two houses have mostly disappeared. The bicameral system now serves mostly to defeat democracy. Having two houses gives Sacramento's huge lobbying corps twice as many dark corners in which to strangle bills they don't like, and twice as many shots at the clandestine last-minute "gut and amend" maneuvers whereby noncontroversial bills are turned into special-interest bonanzas. The two houses wage tit-for-tat wars, sabotaging each other's bills as payback for slights or to gain advantage in the factional battles of Los Angeles Democratic politics.

Around the world, unicameralism is on the march. Even in countries with long histories of having two legislative houses, the old upper house has often become a ceremonial or token presence in lawmaking. In the

United States, Nebraska has had a one-house legislature since 1937, affectionately known as the "Unicam," that is considered a model of civility (it is nonpartisan) and efficiency. Merging the Assembly and State Senate into a single house would provide California the same benefits other unicameral systems enjoy. It would eliminate the cost of maintaining separate committee and leadership staffs in each chamber, simplify and shorten the legislative process, and make it easier for voters to oversee their representatives and hold them accountable.

More important, a unicameral legislature would make it possible to put in place one of the proportional representation models we described above, reforms that would be hard to implement effectively with California's tiny Assembly and Senate. Merging the Assembly and Senate into one house of 120 members would make it possible to implement a multimember district system that has twenty districts with six members each, for example, enough representatives to make proportional representation effective. With a unicameral legislature and a mixed-member system, California could elect eighty lawmakers from single-member districts, just as it does now with the Assembly, while selecting another forty by a statewide party-list vote—a sufficient number to ensure proportional representation and the possible presence of minor parties in the legislature. Creating a California Unicam would be a good reform in itself, but it would also open the door to even better things.

IMPROVED REPRESENTATION

Now we come to the part of the story that few Californians will want to hear. The telling of it brings out the inner five-year-old in many people. They will clap their hands over their ears and shut their eyes tight and chant "nah, nah, nah" in their loudest voice. But for those with more open minds, here is an unwelcome thought to consider: perhaps some of our unhappiness with the legislature is the result of having too few people representing us in Sacramento.

How many legislators does it take to represent nearly 40 million people?

There's no firm rule. As James Madison wrote after the framers puzzled over the issue at the Philadelphia constitutional convention in 1787, "No political problem is less susceptible of a precise solution than that which relates to the number most convenient for a representative legislature."[10] The potential for unhappiness lurks at either extreme. It would hard to find many takers for a legislature of five thousand, roughly the number of lawmakers that would be needed to restore the ratio of representatives to residents set by the California constitution makers of 1879. But few people would think it a good or very democratic idea to reduce the legislature to five members, thereby increasing the population of each district to 8 million. As Madison put it, "by enlarging too much the number of electors, you render the representatives too little acquainted with all their local circumstances and lesser interests."[11] The right answer lies somewhere in the middle.

Right now, California is nowhere close to the middle. The combination of California's relentless population growth and its small legislature has given us the nation's most populous legislative districts. California's Assembly districts each contain about 471,000 persons. Assembly members represent about *three times* as many people as do members of the Texas House of Representatives, which has the next largest lower-house districts, and about *ten times* as many as the average lower-house lawmaker in other states (see Figure 5). If California were a separate nation, its population per lawmaker would be about three times larger than in countries of similar size.[12]

The most remarkable thing about California's status as a leader in representative minimalism is that no one goes around claiming it as a virtue or arguing that California is better governed as a consequence. That's probably because the case would not be easy to make. Minimalism doesn't help achieve any of the things we want in a representative democracy.

For example, we expect that a legislature "should be an exact portrait, in miniature, of the people at large, as it should think, feel, reason and act like them," John Adams wrote at the dawn of the Republic.[13] But a portrait captured in 120 lawmaker-pixels is not a very high-resolution

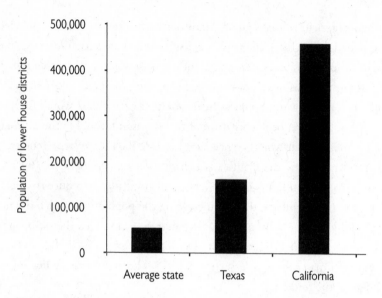

Figure 5   The Size of California Legislative Districts Compared
with Those in Other States. *Source:* Census Bureau, National
Conference of State Legislatures.

image, particularly of a place as varied and complex as California. We
also expect representatives to act in the interests of their constituents. But
gathering the information to understand those interests and translating
that information into an agenda are hard work. That work is not more
likely to get done with fewer hands on the oar. If our idea of representative government involved elevating a cadre of wise guardians to decide
what is good for California, without regard to the views and interests of
constituents, the ratio of lawmakers to citizens would not matter. But
if we believed in such an elitist approach, we would have long ago con-
tracted out lawmaking to radio talk-show gabblers, pundits, and editorial
writers, sparing ourselves the messy business of elections.

Across the political spectrum people believe California representation
falls short of Adams's ideal—that lawmakers "should think, feel, reason
and act like them." Citizens for California Reform, a conservative group
pushing for a part-time "citizen" legislature, says lawmakers "are com-

pletely out of touch with the people they represent." The establishment reform group California Forward seems to agree: it wants to require lawmakers to spend more time in their districts. Both groups believe that citizens' discontent with the legislature can be salved by having legislators spend more time in Pacoima and Patterson and East Oakland.

But the arithmetic does not offer much hope for the effectiveness of such measures. Imagine that the Assembly were in session only twenty weeks a year, with two weeks of vacation, and that your Assembly member spent the remaining forty hours a week, thirty weeks a year, speaking individually to constituents and devoting six minutes to each one. At that breakneck pace, in a two-year term she would succeed in speaking to only one in twenty of the residents of her district. But this is the Internet age, you might object; face-to-face meetings are so twentieth century. So imagine instead that your state senator stays in touch by receiving one Twitter message a year from each of the adults in his district—about a hundred tweets an hour, sixteen hours a day, every day of the year. Every year he would have to read the equivalent of twenty-five books the length of Tolstoy's *War and Peace*!

The groups in Sacramento that get paid by law clients and foundations to cook up "reform" initiatives have good reason to ignore these realities; they are peddling what might get passed, not what will actually work. The rest of us will look instead to both the arithmetic and the very different judgments about district population made around the country and world. If we Californians feel "too little acquainted" with our representatives, and they too little acquainted with us, the fault lies in the numbers and the sheer size of legislative districts.

As a stand-alone issue, reducing the population of districts is the king of political nonstarters. But it needs to be factored into the equation of remaking the legislative branch and how it is elected. California's districts are likely to remain the nation's largest under any political scenario.

Having districts only a bit larger than those in Texas would go far in designing an effective system of proportional representation. It would send to the state capitol a larger group of legislators with a greater variety of ethnic backgrounds, occupations, educational training, and life experiences, the variety needed to represent the most complex society and economy in the nation. That larger membership would require the legislature to have a more robust committee system. Members, no longer required to serve on five or more panels, would develop expertise and have time to conduct more serious oversight of state government, a function that most often takes a back seat.

Such a remade legislature need not be more expensive for taxpayers. Lawmakers could and should be paid lower salaries (they are now the highest in the nation), and they could and should take over work now performed by staff (many of whom now earn more than lawmakers). There is no practical reason why a remade legislature should not be able to live under the existing constitutional cap on appropriations for legislative operations set by voters in 1990 as part of the term limits measure.[14]

A MORE ACCOUNTABLE EXECUTIVE

A legislative branch re-imagined as more democratic, representative, and accountable deserves an equally accountable executive branch as a check and balance. But here we run into another form of political schizophrenia. An extreme minimalist in legislative representation, California leans to excess in state constitutional officers, separately electing eight of them. (Only five other states elect more—North Carolina, North Dakota, Oklahoma, South Carolina, and Washington.) We Californians say we want government to be slim and just get things done; we also want to vote for everything and every office in sight, even if we often don't have a clue who we're voting for and even if the effect is to keep the executive branch of government divided against itself and at odds with our best interests.

The 1996 Constitution Revision Commission addressed California's problem of "knowing who is in charge," politely pointing out all the good-government objections to splitting the management of state government among separately elected and frequently warring officials. The commission drew tidy little boxes explaining which state officers perform independent functions or act as a check and balance—governor, lieutenant governor, attorney general, secretary of state, and controller—and therefore deserved to be elected. It pointed out which officers have only ministerial or regulatory duties—treasurer, superintendent of public instruction, insurance commissioner—and should be appointed by the governor and confirmed by the legislations.

And then the commission's recommendations were just as politely ignored.[15]

So let us be more blunt than a government commission could be. Electing so many statewide officials is not just the path to divided and incoherent government. It's an invitation to sleaze.

Statewide constitutional offices serve mainly as incubators of political ambition. Between 1998 and 2010, all of them except the school superintendent post hatched a candidacy for governor. Ambition in a constitutional officer is not a bad thing in itself. It spurs some to use the tools of the office to do good things for the state that they can later tout on a campaign résumé. But ambition requires money as fuel, and the donors most likely to pump campaign cash to down-ballot officers often have a stake in their decisions. No voters are as interested in the outcome of down-ballot elections as the businesses pushing for a favorable decision at the tax boards, developers angling for tax credits, financial firms wanting a piece of the state's bond business or a slice of the pension funds to manage, public employee unions seeking better benefits through CalPERS, or insurance companies hoping to influence regulation.

The mixture of cash and the official duties of statewide officers has regularly yielded unhappy headlines: School Superintendent Bill Honig was convicted in 1993 of a conflict-of-interest violation for approving contracts with a nonprofit group run by his wife;[16] Controller Gray Davis was found in 1993 handing out probate referee posts, jobs often worth $100,000 a year, to contributors and their families;[17] Insurance Commissioner Chuck Quackenbush was forced to resign in 2000 after giving sweetheart settlements to insurance companies (that had shortchanged earthquake victims) in exchange for contributions that funded TV ads to bolster his political image;[18] Controller Steve Westly pushed the Board of Equalization in 2004 to forgive taxes owed by Barnes & Noble while holding a fund-raiser at the bookseller's New York offices;[19] Secretary of State Kevin Shelley was forced from office in 2005 after a state grant he helped arrange for a nonprofit group ended up in his campaign account.[20] Just as a homeowner learns that letting the frame of his house touch the soil creates a highway for hungry termites, voters have found out that elected down-ballot offices are easy entry points for special interests hungry to feast at public expense.

California's statewide offices fall into three categories:

Obsolete. The lieutenant governor, like the vice president, mostly waits for the governor to die, resign, or get impeached. He casts the tie-breaking vote in the Senate if it's evenly divided, sits on a few boards and commissions that would get along perfectly well without him, and in a throwback to the pre-telephone era, becomes acting governor when the chief executive is out of the state. In Governor Jerry Brown's second term, Lieutenant Governor Mike Curb, a lavishly coiffed but politically inexperienced music mogul selected by Ronald Reagan's "Kitchen Cabinet" to be the Gipper's California heir, used Brown's frequent absences from the state to appoint judges and countermand Brown's policies, delivering comic-opera copy for reporters but something less than good government for the state. At the least, California should elect the governor and lieutenant governor on the same ticket, as the majority of states do. Better yet, it should designate another officer as the governor's emergency successor and join the six states that do nicely without a lieutenant governor.

Appointable. With the obvious exception of the governor, the remaining statewide elected officials perform administrative or regulatory roles, which could be performed just as well by expert appointees. The 1996 Constitution Revision Commission singled out the attorney general, controller, and secretary of state as being worthy of separate election because they play a checking-and-balancing role in government. Its argument was unpersuasive. For example, the attorney general's primary duty is to be the lawyer for the state and the governor. But for much of the past half-century, the governor and the attorney general have come from different parties. The instances in which the attorney general has provided a useful check on the governor are outweighed by the conflicts between them when the attorney general is less than diligent about defending the governor's policies. The federal system—in which the officials responsible for justice, finance, and regulation are appointed by the president, who is responsible for their actions—creates a unified executive branch and clear accountability. During the George W. Bush years, there was no doubt about where to lay the blame for the abuses in the Justice Department or the collapse of the financial sector. Turning most of the statewide offices into gubernatorial appointees, subject to legislative confirmation, would make it clear to Californians who is in charge, reduce partisan conflict within government, and close up some of the cracks that let the special interest termites in.

Electable. The secretary of state is the one exception. Since organizing elections is a state responsibility, there is no federal official corresponding to the California secretary of state, who oversees elections, lobbyists, and the reporting of campaign contributions. The rule here seems fairly obvious: the person who runs the game shouldn't work for the governor, the biggest player. (Which is why people who care about their pocketbooks don't gamble in casinos.) Having a chief elections official elected independently gives voters a way to keep elections free and fair.

As much as we Californians like the idea of having choice, in the end we would be happier with a more accountable and less sleaze-prone state government. So when it comes to electing statewide constitutional offices, two is enough.

BETTER STATEWIDE ELECTIONS

No matter how many executive officers California decides it needs, we can improve the way we elect them by getting rid of the two-step plurality elections for governor and other statewide elected officials in favor of the form of ranked-choice voting known as instant runoff voting (IRV).

Ranked-choice voting is as American as that Oscar-winning blockbuster you watched the other night. It is the system Hollywood now uses to select the winner of the Oscar for best picture, having learned the perils of old-fashioned plurality voting the hard way in 2005. When the envelope for best picture was opened that year, it turned out that George Clooney's *Good Night, and Good Luck* had split the high-minded historical-drama vote with Steven Spielberg's *Munich*, and that *Brokeback Mountain* had split the gay vote with *Capote*. Those splits let the guilty-liberal vote push *Crash* to a plurality victory. A majority of the voters would doubtless have preferred any of the other candidates to *Crash*, whose box office receipts (the lowest in modern history for any Oscar winner) signaled the movie audience's own feelings.

A first-past-the-post election had undermined the interests of both art and commerce. To prevent that from happening again, the motion picture academy switched in 2009 to ranked-choice voting, allowing Hollywood to hand out nominations to ten movies safe in the knowledge that the Oscar would be awarded to a picture with majority appeal.

Members now get to express their differing tastes. And in the end they get a winner that a majority of them can live with.

An instant runoff election for California's executive leaders would work in the same way to select winners with the broadest appeal to the state's voters. Under IRV there would be only one statewide election, instead of a primary election followed months later by a general election. All the candidates for governor (as well as any other statewide elected offices California wants to retain) would appear on one ballot. Voters would then rank the candidates, designating a first choice, a second choice, and so on down the list.

After the polling, election officials would count the ballots, tallying all the top-choice votes. If one candidate had a majority of votes, she would be declared the winner. Otherwise, the candidate with the fewest votes would be eliminated and his ballots would be assigned according to his voters' second-choice candidates. Then the votes would be tallied again to determine if a candidate had a majority. The count would continue in this way, with the last-place candidate eliminated and his votes reassigned, until one candidate emerged with a majority. In place of two expensive elections held five months apart, IRV provides a way to hold a virtual series of runoff elections in a single day to yield a winner with majority support.

IRV helps with all the major problems in our current electoral system:

1. There would be no more "spoilers" to split the vote and deliver a plurality victory to a candidate opposed by the majority. If Florida had used IRV in the 2000 presidential election, it is reasonable to assume that most voters who cast their ballots for Ralph Nader would have made Al Gore their second choice. When no candidate received a majority, Nader's second-place votes would have been reassigned, making Gore a clear winner and sparing the country the divisive spectacle of having George W. Bush elected president despite having lost the national popular vote.

2. IRV would accomplish the goal of primary reformers—providing centrist candidates access to the general election ballot—without infringing the First Amendment rights of parties or denying voters choices at the general election, as in a top-two primary.

In fact, under IRV more voters would have more choice—major-party candidates, minor-party candidates, independents—and they could exercise it without fear of wasting their votes. If they were dissatisfied with the candidates offered by the Democrats and Republicans, they would be free to send that signal by voting for a minor-party candidate. But they would still potentially have a voice in selecting the winner of the election with their second- or third-place votes if no candidate received a majority in the first round. Freed of the worry of wasting their votes, many more Californians would be able to express their true preferences in elections. Even if their first choice were defeated, their vote would send an important signal that the major parties were not addressing concerns important to many voters.

3. Under IRV, statewide election campaigns would be less polarizing and less negative. The current system of primaries and winner-take-all elections is responsible for the familiar complaint that politicians speak with forked tongues.

In the primary campaign, a candidate must spend all his time, effort, and money convincing his party's base voters that he, and not the other guys, is the true Democrat or the true disciple of Ronald Reagan—or failing that, less of an unethical scoundrel. His goal is simply to be one vote more appealing than anyone else. Once the primary is over, however, the winner must then turn around and assure the rest of the electorate—particularly voters in the middle, many of whom have been looking on as the primary campaign played out noisily over the airwaves—not to take seriously anything he said in the previous three months. He must convince them to ignore everything he said about his uncompromisingly partisan beliefs or about his primary election opponents, all of whom, it now turns out, are wonderful people who will be supporting him in November, no matter all the nasty things they said about one another in the spring. A system that requires politicians to be two-faced to be successful does not invite public trust in leaders.

Instant-runoff voting changes these dynamics for the better. Imagine yourself one of the multiple candidates running in an IRV election for an open position as governor or treasurer. You know from polling that no candidate is likely to win outright in the first round; the votes will be split widely among the four or more major-party candidates. To win, you will need not only to be ranked first by many voters, but also to attract the second- and third-place rankings on the ballots cast for your rivals. Now ask yourself a few questions. Do you think it will be a winning strategy to alienate the majority of voters who don't make you their first choice by launching negative attacks on the candidate they prefer? Do you want to harp on your unswerving loyalty to your party's core values if you need second-place votes from voters of the other party? Politics in California under IRV would be painted in a color scheme more nuanced than red and blue, or black and white.[21]

4. Statewide elections using IRV would reduce the cost of campaigning and the influence of large donors. Running for statewide office in California, with its 38 million people and eleven television markets, is hugely expensive. The three major gubernatorial candidates in 2006 spent more than $130 million in the primary and general elections. The money came either from the checks they wrote to themselves—former state controller Steve Westly threw $35 million of his own money into an unsuccessful primary campaign—or from thousands of hours they spent on the telephone or in meetings with the wealthiest Californians, feeding the donors' already plump egos and listening to their complaints about how hard the rich have it. The nicest thing you can say about this money chase is that it does not give our prospective leaders a broad acquaintance with the circumstances and hopes of ordinary Californians. IRV would not take the money out of politics, of course. But statewide candidates would have to raise money for only one statewide contest instead of two, which would represent an improvement, both in candidates' sanity and in the public interest.

The most common criticism of IRV is that it is too unfamiliar and complicated for voters. "It makes such radical assumptions about how people make choices," said an IRV opponent shortly before voters in St. Paul, Minnesota, adopted the system in 2009. "We choose yes/no, we don't rank."[22] Such critics have apparently never visited the Internet. Ranked-choice voting—in surveys, product and film reviews, dating sites—is everywhere online. Marking ballots with ranked choices in California elections requires no intellectual stretch for voters. Australia and Ireland have used it for nearly a century in national and state elections, and it has been adopted by both St. Paul and Minneapolis in Minnesota and by municipalities from Vermont to Colorado. IRV has been used in San Francisco city elections since 2004 and has been approved by voters in Oakland, Berkeley, and Davis.

In 2005, when San Francisco first used IRV to elect the low-profile citywide offices of city assessor and treasurer, only about half the voters knew before voting that they would be asked to rank their choices. Yet 87 percent of them reported afterward that they understood the system "perfectly well" or "fairly well," and told surveyors by a three-to-one margin that they preferred IRV to the old two-election model. Support for the old way was concentrated heavily among the elderly and very elderly. And therein lies the story: only blind adherence to tradition and fear of the unfamiliar stand between California, home of innovation, and an electoral system that represents an important and democratic advance over plurality elections and first-past-the-post.[23]

8

GOVERNMENT
FROM THE BOTTOM UP

California has never squarely faced the question of scale. "The experts now forecast that California will show an additional gain of 2,650,000 in the 1950s," Carey McWilliams wrote in 1949 about the state's burgeoning postwar population. "It is expected that 20 million people will eventually reside within its boundaries."[1] His experts were off target by only a factor of two. California would add 5.1 million new residents in the fifties. "Eventually" has not yet arrived, but the state had 38 million people within its boundaries by the beginning of 2009, on its way to almost 60 million by 2050.[2]

Despite his clouded crystal ball, McWilliams captured California's enduring ambivalence about growth. "Californians, of course, are fascinated by facts and figures showing the state's phenomenal growth and yet, on the other side of their minds, they are disturbed and even repelled by these same figures," he wrote. "They want the state to grow, and yet they don't want it to grow."[3] The ambivalence can be measured today with a simple Google search. Type in the query "'eighth largest economy in the world' California" and Google will throw back more than 400,000 links, many of them telling of the pride Californians take that their state operates at a global scale. Type in the query "'thirty-fifth largest population in the world' California" and only a couple of hits come back. Californians enjoy their economic lifting power but would prefer to ignore how many biceps it takes to hoist California to such riches. "They like the idea of growth and expansion," McWilliams wrote, "but withdraw from the practical implications."[4]

California still lives within the boundaries of the state for which the 1879 constitution was written. It is not, however, the same place. A delegate to the 1878–79 convention, had he wished to ponder the work before him, might have climbed to the peak of Mt. Diablo in the East Bay and, on a clear day, overlooked almost two-thirds of the state's population. Their numbers then would fit comfortably into today's San Jose, with room left over for all of Pasadena.

Neither is California the same place where Hiram Johnson campaigned in 1910, crisscrossing the state in his crimson Locomobile and ringing a cowbell at every stop to draw a crowd. The Progressive reforms of direct democracy were approved in a state with the same population as Wisconsin, about 2.3 million.

Over the following decade California would grow by roughly the equivalent of a Connecticut. In the 1920s it would add a Virginia. The pace slowed a bit in the Depression decade: California grew by only a Colorado and a Delaware. McWilliams wrote about California's ambivalence to growth at the end of a decade in which California had added a North Carolina. And then things really picked up: a Tennessee and an Arkansas in the fifties; a Louisiana and a Maine in the sixties; a Minnesota in the seventies. In the three decades since Prop 13 centralized power at the state capitol, California has grown by the equivalent of a whole Texas.[5]

California may think of itself as a kind of quasi-nation with, in historian Kevin Starr's eight-volume telling, its very own dream.[6] It has yet to shape its government, though, to a form consistent with its size and complexity. Countries of California's heft almost universally govern themselves through some form of federal system, with power shared between a central government and elected regional governments fitted to places that form natural communities by virtue of their shared geography, economy, or ethnicity. California still tries to muddle through with government institutions that owe their DNA to that nineteenth-century Iowa constitution from which the forty-niners so freely cribbed.

California is a nation without states. Its central government in Sacramento seems, to many of us, too distant to understand our needs. Its local governments are often scaled at the wrong size and are deprived of the tools and flexibility to effectively solve the problems that touch our everyday lives, such as crime and schools. What was true in McWilliams's time remains true today: the ambivalence about growth "consistently undercuts any attempt to plan for the well-being of Californians, present and future." The whole system requires a Great Unwinding.[7]

ONE, TWO, THREE, MANY CALIFORNIAS

When Californians get around to considering that maybe their state has outgrown its institutions, it is usually during hard times and in the form of the most apocalyptic, and most unserious, idea: splitting California into several states.

In early 2009, during the depths of the Great Recession, Bill Maze, a former Republican member of the Assembly from Visalia, launched a campaign, called Downsize California, to cleave the state, east from west. "We have to ask ourselves, Is there a better way to govern this state?" Maze said. The precipitating event for this attempted divorce, according to its sponsors, a group of disgruntled agriculturists, was the passage of Proposition 2, a 2008 initiative written by the Humane Society of the United States to regulate agribusiness's caging of chickens, calves, and pigs. Maze drew a map splitting off thirteen coastal counties, from Marin to Los Angeles, to form a new state. He left the other forty-five counties as the "real" California, inhabited by what he called "normal people." His aim was to qualify an initiative to divorce his two Californias for the 2012 ballot. The folks on the coast "think fish are more important than people, that pigs are treated mean and chickens should run loose," Virgil Rogers, a retired dairyman and chairman of Maze's downsizing group, told the *New York Times*. (So, apparently, does a majority in their "real" California, where Prop 2 and its protections for chickens won 59 percent of the vote.)[8]

This is familiar territory for Californians. Kevin Starr counts two hundred efforts to divide the state, beginning with a quickly dismissed 1849 idea that California enter the Union as two states, one slave, one free.[9] Motorists who traverse the fish-and-forest counties of the state's far north can see lingering signs of the push, at the end of the Depression, to break off those counties as a new state called Jefferson.

In the jarring recession of the early 1990s, Stan Statham, the former TV news reader who represented the northern state in the Assembly, proposed to split California into three states, north, central, and south. The proposal—which went on the ballot as an advisory measure in thirty-one counties and was approved in twenty-seven—lost momentum when the boom years returned. The pattern seems set: dizzying growth and change roil the state. Californians' increasing variety strains their common bonds. Hard times trigger thoughts of breakup. The divorce effort falters, undone by the return of prosperity and by the ridicule of those in the political arena.

Maze's idea of splitting California east and west was quickly smothered in hilarity. The inland state could be called "Appalachifornia," journalist Peter Schrag wrote, and make its living by expensively selling its water and renting out its prison cells to its former mates on the coast. How would inland California—"a new flyover state stripped of some of the world's most profitable industries and most exclusive property"—pay for schools and other services? Bill McEwen, a *Fresno Bee* columnist asked his readers, prospective residents of a new inland California. "This idea only works if the 51st state—drawn to be conservative to the core—legalizes marijuana."[10]

The laughter directed at such proposals is well deserved but shouldn't drown out two important things the state splitters know.

The first is that there are one, two, three, many Californias. Californians are not Badgers or Tar Heels. They may all live on a piece of ground labeled "California" on the map, but they don't have the common traditions of cultural belonging and history that shape most other states. They are tugged apart by ethnicity and class. They are spread across an enormous expanse of topography and climate, most of them in one of a half-dozen distinct urban regions, each of which is more populous than many states. They share institutions of government but not a true political community; they are more defined by their conflicts and alienation than by the values they have in common—unless you count their devotion to the inflexible initiative process and other sources of governing dysfunction. They sometimes get out of their own regions to mingle at the state's public universities and in its prisons. But unlike the residents of many states, they have no dominant newspaper or statewide broadcast outlets to share the news and debate their future together.

If you listen to the state's political talk, you would guess that the one thing that surely ties Californians together is the economy. Politicians promise they know how to "grow the California economy." They wring their hands over the "California business climate." But economists will tell you that there is no such thing as a single "California economy" or "California business climate." Regions, with well-defined labor markets and distinctive clusters of goods and services producers, are natural economic units. So are nations, with their control over currencies and trade. States are not.

The economies of California's regions each move at their own pace and with their own mix of industries. The Bay Area got clobbered by the collapse of the dot-com bubble and the 2001 recession; Los Angeles was barely touched. The collapse of the housing bubble in 2008 hit inland California harder than the coast. Unemployment rates in the ensuing recession varied almost as much between the state's regions as they did between California and other states. The Central Valley, which would rank forty-eighth among the states in per capita income, is as economically different from the San Francisco Bay Area as Mississippi is from Massachusetts. The northern part of the state has as little in common with Los Angeles as Wyoming does with New York City.[11]

The other thing the splitters know is that California is not organized to cope with either the state's size or the differing needs of its distinct regions. "We'd be better off if we had more say in what we do," Curt Hubbard, a north state rancher said in 1993, during Stan Statham's push to divide California. "It . . . would help to split the state." He was wrong about splitting the state—it would create more problems than it would solve, and Congress would never approve. But he was right that giving Californians more say in governing themselves locally would make everyone—except maybe the lobbyists in Sacramento—better off.[12]

THE COMMONSENSE SOLUTION

There is no secret about how to restore local control and flexibility to California government. Since 1993 the formula has rested on the shelves of policy wonks all over Sacramento, gathering dust.

Nineteen ninety-three was a tough year in California. The state's economy had been hit by a double whammy: a recession and the post–Cold War downsizing of the state's huge defense and aerospace industries. The budget was badly out of balance. Local and state government were at war because state policy makers, desperate to fill the state's fiscal hole, were pulling back the bailout money they had given to cities and counties after Prop 13. Voters were in a sour mood, unhappy with their legislature and with cuts in public services, and ready to blame the scarcity on unauthorized immigrants.

Into this malaise, the legislature's nonpartisan analyst, Elizabeth Hill, and her staff tossed a big idea for untangling the mess of governments that so baffle Californians and prevent them from holding their elected leaders accountable for results.

Titled "Making Government Make Sense," the twenty-page chapter in the legislative analyst's annual policy document offered what it modestly described as "a model of a rational organization for our system of government." At the heart of that model was an understanding that a state of California's size couldn't be effectively governed from the top down.[13] The author of the 1993 paper, Peter Schaafsma, who was at that time the director for state and local finance in the Legislative Analyst's Office (LAO), had been thinking through these issues for years. The inadvertent Great Centralization created by Prop 13 had taken away local flexibility. It had lodged power in the legislature, where interest groups held sway and "the notion that programs are expected to work is a foreign concept," Schaafsma said. "I had a nexus in mind about how to sort it out. And it was consistent with what we'd been working on internally. We thought somebody needed to say this."[14]

What the LAO said in 1993 applies with just as much force today. The things about government that drive Californians crazy—the unending war of capture-the-dollars between state and local government; the local governments doling out six-figure pensions at a time when the state is taking away kids' health insurance coverage and shutting students out of college; the proliferation of agencies no one understands or can hold accountable—"are inherent to our system, and stem from its failure to assign responsibilities clearly among government agencies and provide them with the authority and tools to get their jobs done," the LAO wrote.[15]

The changes needed are fundamental, yet they involve no more than common sense: (1) the duty to run each major program should be assigned to the proper level of government; (2) along with each duty should come control over the revenue needed to carry it out; and (3) the focus should be on achieving the results taxpayers want—safer streets, better schools, healthier lives—with fiscal rewards for success and costs for failure.

Which level of government should do what? The sorting isn't too hard. In education, only the state can provide the equalized school funding required by the courts and the student achievement standards required by federal law. But decisions about how to use that money in ways that yield the greatest amount of learning are properly made as close to the kids as possible. The state is the natural home for the public universities, the courts, health care, and the safety net that keeps the elderly poor, the disabled, and the jobless from plunging into poverty. Local government is the natural home for the services directly related to people's homes (fire protection, zoning, code enforcement) and for the community-based services that prevent and punish crime and promote social order (police, probation, jails, substance abuse treatment, child protective services, mental health).

The difficult parts of making government make sense are ensuring that the revenue goes along with program responsibility and that the level of government given a duty has the flexibility to do what really works. Those changes require political will to overcome inertia and vested interests. A quick look at how the model could be applied to reducing crime will show, however, that the fight is worth having.

GOVERNING FOR LESS CRIME

Controlling crime is a big business in California. State and local governments spent a total of roughly $34 billion, or about $900 per capita, on criminal justice in 2006–07. The only greater government expense was schools. About a third of these dollars were spent by the state for prisons, courts, and substance-abuse control. Local governments spent the rest, largely for police, prosecutors, probation, and jails.

This huge outlay reflects a rare double consensus in the state's political life. Californians widely agree that crime control is a core function of government. And they widely agree on the outcome they want—fewer crimes. Crime is costly to society—the tab probably runs about $130 billion a year in California—and the costs of crime fall most heavily on poorer people and neighborhoods with the fewest economic and civic resources. Reducing crime serves both justice and social justice.[16]

Having agreed on first principles and the outcome they seek, Californians are free to ask more pragmatic questions. Does California get the greatest possible benefit from the investment it makes in fighting crime? Might spending their criminal justice tax dollars on a different mix of activities work better? Could additional dollars spent in the right way reduce crime more? A lot rides on the answers. If a more effective use of current or additional criminal justice dollars were to yield even a 10 percent reduction in crime, the economic benefit would amount to more than the state now spends on its two public university systems.

In fact, the evidence suggests that California isn't putting its crime-fighting dollars in the right places. Mark Kleiman, a professor and criminal justice expert at UCLA, shows in his book *When Brute Force Fails* that the emphasis, in California and elsewhere, on long prison terms has diminishing returns in reducing crime. Crime is a young man's game, but a large share of prison dollars is spent warehousing middle-aged criminals—half of California's inmates are over 35. "Our prisons are filled with people who would otherwise be retired—or at least semi-retired—offenders," Kleiman writes, "not worth the prison space they occupy." The dollars used to confine them, if spent in smarter ways, could provide greater crime reduction. "Theory and evidence agree: swift and certain punishment, even if not severe, will control the vast bulk of offending behavior." Putting more resources into strategically targeted policing and into probation (the latter overhauled to make it effective in monitoring and controlling the behavior of offenders) could lead to both less crime and less punishment, Kleiman argues.[17]

If Kleiman is right, how can communities in California get to the balance of investments he recommends? They probably can't under California's current governing custom of divorcing duties and dollars. Cities that want to try out Kleiman's approach can't choose to shift dollars from incarceration to policing because the state sets criminal sentences and funds prisons. Counties don't have control over their revenue, making new investments in transformed probation unlikely. The criminal justice system has so divided responsibilities that it can't be managed to achieve the outcomes all of us agree on.

Here's where the "making government make sense" model shines. It would make possible the kind of cost-effective choices the current system prevents.

Under the model, both the responsibility and the money for crime control would be handed to cities. They would be free to use them in the most cost-effective way. Communities could still send offenders to prison, which the state would continue to operate, but they would be required to pay the state for renting the cells, at prices that now run almost $50,000 a year per inmate. As the legislative analyst put it in 1993, "the high costs of this alternative would provide an incentive for them to explore local options." Each community, looking at its own particular needs, would search for the right balance of policing, probation (the service would be bought from the counties), jail, treatment for mental illness and substance abuse, and prison.[18]

The model would offer not only flexibility, but also the right incentives to use it well. A city that spent its dollars wisely on strategies that reduced crime would have to spend less on punishment. That would free up more money to reinvest in the successful strategies. With less of the crime that cripples neighborhoods and drives away businesses, such a city would gain investment and jobs, which would provide more revenue. Success would be rewarded, in a virtuous circle. In the same way, bad decisions would have consequences. A community that took the wrong path would end up with high rates of crime and a citizenry wanting to know why their leaders had failed to do as well as the neighboring city down the road. The model makes for the kind of accountability the current system, with its separation of revenue and responsibility, lacks.

The stress on performance would extend all the way to Sacramento. Prisons would no longer get business by default. They would be selling their services—incapacitation and rehabilitation—to local government customers that would have the flexibility to make choices about the best way to spend their money. How long could the state prison system continue to sell an expensive service that warehouses inmates for years, then returns them to society without treating their drug and mental health problems or giving them basic education and job skills?

RIGHT-SIZING LOCAL GOVERNMENT

The idea of making government make sense raises its own question of scale. California is too big and teeming to have all its decisions made at the state capitol. But it also has too many local governments—and too many of them of the wrong size—to cope intelligently with problems like crime.

California is barnacled in governments. It has fifty-eight counties, ranging in population from 1,201 (Alpine) to 10.4 million (Los Angeles). It has 478 cities and 425 redevelopment agencies. It has seventy-two community college boards and 1,050 school districts. It has 4,778 special districts, 2,998 of them independently elected or appointed, covering everything from birth (hospital districts) to death (cemetery districts). This profusion owes nothing to intelligent design. "I currently have twenty-two people I elect to represent me at all levels of government, and I can't name them—and I'm president of the California Voter Foundation," Kim Alexander, the leader of the civic education group said in 2009.[19]

At the local level, the Great Unwinding of this mess of governments inevitably must be an extinction event. Hundreds, perhaps thousands, of special districts need to go the way of the dinosaurs.

Many independent special districts that provide a single service, like fire protection or park operations, receive a guaranteed share of property tax revenue. Their funding bears no relationship to either the actual cost of delivering that service or its value to the community. Operating largely out of public view, with little scrutiny from the media, special districts in recent years have yielded one scandal after another—pension spiking, personal use of public funds, runaway salaries.

In its 1993 proposal to make government make sense, the legislative analyst urged that special districts' property tax dollars be funneled through their counties or cities, which would fund them as needed or take them over. In that way, special districts would get the oversight they now lack. County and city boards, which are more visible and accountable to voters, would weigh the value of special district services against other community priorities. Much of a whole layer of government would disappear, and many redundant agencies, from park districts to levee maintenance districts, could be eliminated through consolidation.[20]

Getting rid of dinosaurs is a start, but meeting the needs of a fast-changing state requires acts of local government creation and evolution too. In the late 1980s, with the state choking on urban sprawl and congestion, there was a push for more regional governance, to plan for transportation, housing, and resources across whole regional economies. Assembly Speaker Willie Brown even sponsored a bill to set up regional governments. But the regionalization push and Brown's bill foundered when recession briefly stopped growth and local governments fought back to preserve their power.

There are examples of regional and collaborative governance. California's biggest success—the South Coast Air Quality Management District, which regulates the Los Angeles air basin, and other regional air boards set up to reduce smog—has been a case of a broadly and intensely shared regional interest (in breathing) overcoming squabbles about local turf and power. In more recent years, each of the four biggest metropolitan regions, pushed by their own residents, conducted "blueprint" planning—public dialogues on how local governments might coordinate growth policies.[21]

The lesson is that local government evolution is more likely to come not from on high, but from the bottom up, in response to citizen pressure. The issue is how to make such evolution easier. One of the best recommendations of the last Constitution Revision Commission—the thoughtful, if ignored, 1996 effort—was to give citizens in California's different regions both the permission and the tools to remake their local agencies and take more control over their destiny. Under the commission's proposal, counties and groups would be empowered (but not required) to set up citizen commissions to rethink their local governments—shuffle and combine their missions, merge or eliminate them, redraw their boundaries. Out of these deliberations would come a new charter for voter approval, and a restoration of the promise of home rule that was part of the 1879 constitution.[22]

What might governments remade to make sense look like? The answers could be different in every region. The more rural parts of the state, with their lagging agricultural economies and deep poverty, might better organize themselves to improve education and spur new kinds of investment and jobs. The residents of Los Angeles County might consider, among many other things, whether a board of supervisors with only five members is the right way to govern more than 10 million people.

The Californians who feel no kinship with other parts of the state and see no other path but splitting the state would get the best part of what they want: more say in their own local affairs, with institutions they and their neighbors design for themselves, scale to their own communities, and bend to their wishes at the polls.

TAKING LOCAL CONTROL SERIOUSLY

In 1993, when the Legislative Analyst's Office put out its ideas for how to make government in California make sense, there was "a lot of interest," said Peter Schaafsma, author of the report. Local control is something most people across the political spectrum accept, at least in principle. The legislative analyst's proposal particularly excited local government officials, weighed down as they were by the centralized Prop 13 operating system. "I went out on the rubber-chicken circuit. Everyone wanted to talk about it," Schaafsma said. But the idea quickly got filed on the shelf, the same fate that would soon befall the home-rule recommendations of the 1996 constitutional revision commission. "Nobody wanted to do anything," Schaafsma said. Any proposal to restore more responsibility to local governments in California must first punch through the armies of vested interests protecting the state capitol's power and privileges. "Sacramento is an intransigent place," Schaafsma said. "So many interest groups don't want change."[23]

Under the current system, interest groups don't have to make their cases to voters and elected officials in hundreds of different local venues. They can take the steam out of grassroots movements, as when business and health organizations in 1994 made a deal to have the state preempt regulation of indoor smoking and snuff out the successful citizen-driven campaign that had passed local antismoking ordinances protecting two-thirds of the state's workers.[24] When it's a choice between the golden principle of local control or the hard nugget of policy gain that can be mined in Sacramento, count on interest groups choosing the gold they can put in their pockets.

The other obstacle to local control is money. A big part of giving Californians more say in what their local governments do is giving them a bigger say about how much those governments raise, and a larger revenue stake in the success or failure of those choices.

"The ability of local agencies to determine the appropriate mix and level of expenditures to reflect their community's preferences is dependent upon the community's ability to raise—or lower—the level of local taxes they pay," the LAO said in 1993.[25] Its plan proposed letting local voters, by majority vote, change the Prop 13-mandated 1 percent property tax rate (but not the Prop 13 assessment cap protecting homeowners from housing inflation). The 1996 constitution revision commission also called for letting voters in their new charter governments raise taxes, other than property taxes, by majority vote.

The usual response to such proposals is to yell, "Protect Prop 13!" The tactic usually works. Although few Californians know exactly what it says or how it has centralized government, Prop 13 is the best brand in California politics. To most voters, the phrase "Prop 13" means one thing, and one thing only: certainty about their property tax bill. The point of yelling "Protect Prop 13" is not to inform people, but to end any conversation. Invoking Prop 13 is how politicians wave the bloody shirt in California's ideological civil war.

But Prop 13 is not a single thing. It is a bundle of policies: a uniform 1 percent property tax rate; assessments set at the time of sale; a 2 percent annual cap on increases in assessments; the ban on real estate transfer taxes; legislative apportionment of property tax revenues; supermajority vote requirements for the legislature to increase revenues and for local voters to approve taxing themselves for specific purposes. It is possible to have the best of Prop 13—the insurance policy to keep inflation from driving up property taxes beyond homeowners' ability to pay—while changing the Prop 13 operating system that has weakened local control, led to centralized government, and abandoned local government to public employees.

One of the many ironies of California politics is that those for whom Prop 13 is an article of faith are often the same people who shout loudest that state government is too big and that local control is essential. The Prop 13 operating system is, after all, big government in the extreme. It establishes one-size-fits-all governance for every community in a state that is larger and more varied than any other. If local control means anything, it means letting local elected leaders and voters make their own—and probably very different—choices about how much revenue to raise to meet their local needs. Government in California can't be made to make sense without taking local control seriously.

9

A MORE DIRECT DEMOCRACY

Darrell Steinberg had to decide whether to betray himself.

In February 2009, Steinberg led the California State Senate as its president pro tem. But he was locked in negotiations that made him feel like a hostage. The country's economic collapse had caused a historic collapse in tax revenues. California faced a budget deficit in the tens of billions. The state had no cash in its main accounts and had already raided more than 650 of the special funds scattered around the treasury to pay its bills. The world's credit markets were so damaged that borrowing short-term cash was prohibitively expensive. By late February, California would be out of cash. The state controller was preparing to pay bills with IOUs.

Steinberg desperately wanted to balance the budget. But every political option was blocked, many of them by previous ballot initiatives. The Democratic majority was willing to raise taxes, but Republicans, using the leverage of Prop 13's requirement of a two-thirds vote to do so, were balking. Politically, the safest approach was to cut health and human services programs, but that had two big drawbacks. First, it would put holes in the safety net programs during bad economic times—precisely when people needed them most. Second, since state spending on health and human services programs is matched with federal funds, cuts would pull dollars out of the California economy, deepening the recession.

As negotiators searched for money, Republicans suggested diverting tax dollars from two popular programs, early childhood services and mental health. These programs were rare birds. Each was established by a ballot initiative (Proposition 10 in 1998 for early childhood; Proposition 63 in 2004 for mental health). And neither was the sort of "something for nothing" measure so common on the California ballot. To the contrary, each initiative had enacted a new, dedicated source of tax revenue to fund its programs (tobacco taxes for early childhood; an income tax surcharge on millionaires for mental health). Because they had been established by voters, these programs existed outside the normal budget process. And because they were running a big surplus, they were tempting targets for lawmakers short on cash. In negotiations, legislative leaders debated taking roughly half of those surpluses: $1.6 billion over five years from early childhood and more than $500 million over two years from mental health.

This was dangerous territory for Steinberg personally. Not only were such programs a top priority for his party and its donor base, but Steinberg himself had been the author of Prop 63, the initiative that established the tax for mental health. Unable to get such a tax through the Assembly when he chaired the budget committee there, he had, like any interest group, taken his case to the people, and scored a victory. Prop 63 was the signature achievement of Steinberg's career. It had given him statewide notoriety and was one reason why he was leading the State Senate.

Steinberg thus faced the choice: do his job or preserve his record. The Republican legislative leaders were willing to put up enough votes for a budget that included temporary tax increases. This act of GOP responsibility was also a political risk, a violation of anti-tax orthodoxy in a party that had grown smaller and more conservative. As part of their price for the tax increase, the Republicans asked Steinberg to take his own risk. Steinberg also saw that if he didn't go along the outcome would be perverse: the state would be cutting basic health programs even as it allowed these two initiative-protected programs to maintain surpluses. Reluctantly, he agreed to take money from his own program, as well as from early childhood services.

"We were faced with a $41 billion deficit and a political system where it's next to impossible to raise taxes through the legislative process," Steinberg would later say. "But I had a different responsibility, a responsibility as leader in the legislature to set an example. As we were asking others, including Republicans, to violate their own orthodoxy, I couldn't say, 'You can look at everything except what's important to me.' I didn't like it, but I had to support it."[1]

A deal was reached, but that wasn't the end of the story. In every other state in the union, the legislative agreement to take the funds would have closed the matter. In California, that was not enough. Steinberg might be the leader of the majority in the upper house of the legislature. He might be the author of the program he had reluctantly agreed to raid. But an initiative couldn't simply be changed by elected leaders or its author; there had to be another vote of the people. The initiative process exists in a world all its own, beyond checks and balances. So the best the legislature could do was draw up two ballot measures—Propositions 1D and 1E—to get voter approval before the money could be used to balance the budget.

It wasn't enough for Steinberg to betray himself; he'd have to get permission first.

WHY THE VOTERS HAVE TO VOTE

There could be no better illustration than Steinberg himself of how California's legislative branch had become hopelessly and inflexibly divided against itself. Steinberg had a foot on both sides of the divide—as a legislator and as the author of a successful initiative—but not even he could straddle this chasm.

In May 2009, Californians would cast ballots on Propositions 1D and 1E—plus four other compromise measures that came out of the same desperate negotiations to change the budget before the state ran out of cash. The six measures did not exist because a majority of legislators wanted them on the ballot. Lawmakers would have been happy to enact the deal themselves without having to ask voters. The measures were all there because California's system had forced lawmakers' hand.

Proposition 1A was a compromise—forced on the Democratic majority by the handful of Republicans who agreed to vote for the deal and reach the two-thirds threshold—to raise taxes temporarily in exchange for the establishment of a rainy-day fund. Proposition 1F, a populist measure to tie legislative pay to budget timing, was another Republican demand enacted only because of the two-thirds leverage. Proposition 1B resulted from a deal with the teachers' unions, using the leverage that Proposition 98 provided them, that permitted short-term budget cuts in exchange for revised funding formulas to boost education spending over the long term. Proposition 1C, which sought to borrow against future lottery proceeds, had to go on the ballot because it altered the 1984 ballot initiative that created the lottery.

Voters were themselves responsible for the existence of these ballot measures, but Californians went to the polls grudgingly, blaming the legislature for sticking them with the responsibility of choosing. Surveys showed that significant blocs of voters—one-third of those surveyed by Field in April 2009 and 50 percent of Republicans in the poll—were opposing all measures on the ballot at least in part because they thought the legislature shouldn't have been bothering voters with these questions—despite the constitutional requirement that voters be bothered. (This absence of self-awareness among the California electorate has a long history. In 1978 a group wrote a ballot argument in verse that objected to a measure to change the state chiropractic board on the grounds that the legislature, by putting the issue on the ballot, was wasting voters' time. Unfortunately, it was a constitutionally required waste of time, because the state law on chiropractors had been created by initiative in 1922).[2]

Surveying the results of the May 2009 election, Field Poll Director Mark DiCamillo concluded: "Voters feel the Legislature isn't doing its job, hasn't been able to work with the governor and is just passing these things on to them."[3] This mood prevailed. Five of the six measures were defeated, with only Prop 1F, the populist blast at legislative pay, winning.

The failed special election was one more casualty of the cycle of con-tempt produced by the initiative process. The public distrusts the legisla-ture and their elected officials. So voters, preferring to trust themselves, make major policy decisions via ballot initiative. These decisions, because of the requirement that initiatives not be changed by legislators alone, further tie the hands of lawmakers. The frustrated lawmakers find it difficult to solve pressing problems, further fueling the public frustration that produces more initiatives and more hand-tying. This vicious cycle produces anger, more budgeting at the ballot box, and poor governance.

This system also defies accountability. Who is really responsible for the problems of lawmaking and budgeting in California? Lawmakers, with good reason, can blame the voters, who have reduced their ability to come up with solutions. Voters, with good reason, can blame the law-makers, who after all have high-paying jobs and plenty of time to balance budgets but never seem able to do so.

The blame game is played endlessly. The fact that there is never a clear winner is precisely the problem. The legislature and the voters each legislate. They are part of the same branch of government. But these two halves of the branch are not linked together in any meaningful way. California's system puts lawmakers and voters on entirely separate tracks—even though they are shaping the same laws and the same con-stitution. The legislative branch is unaccountable precisely because it is divided in this way.

THE WORLD'S MOST INFLEXIBLE INITIATIVE PROCESS

There are no data to suggest that our legislators are lesser beings than those who haunt statehouses and congresses and parliaments the world over. And California is not the only place with direct democracy. Twenty-four states have some form of initiative at the state level. All fifty states offer direct democracy at the local level. And more than a hundred of the world's countries permit direct democracy at the state or local level.[4]

Switzerland, the only country with a federal system of direct democracy (a system that inspired the Progressives who adopted initiative and referendum in California), is among the world's best governed, least corrupt, and most peaceful nations.

What makes California different? It's the design of the state's system of direct democracy, and in particular, its initiative process.

Specifically, California has the most powerful—and thus the most inflexible—initiative process in the world. The legislature has no constitutional power to stop an initiative from reaching the ballot. Nor does the governor or any member of the executive branch. Judicial authorities can block initiatives with constitutional infirmities, but precedent sets a high standard for doing so. In all twenty-three other states with the initiative process, legislatures may change a law enacted by initiative. Sometimes, there is a waiting period of two years before lawmakers can act, or maybe a supermajority is required to make a change. California is the only state where a statute enacted by initiative can only be undone with another popular vote (unless the original initiative permits legislative amendment).[5]

Initiatives to amend the constitution present a similar problem. A constitutional amendment put to the voters by an initiative requires only a simple majority of votes to pass. But if the legislature wants to amend or revise the constitution, it must muster a two-thirds vote—and then win the approval of the voters.

These incentives give California's direct democracy the strongest pro-initiative bias of any such system in the world. The other tools of direct democracy have fallen into disuse. The recall is uncommon; the 2003 recall of Governor Gray Davis was the first of a statewide elected official. The referendum is rarely used—fewer than seventy-five have been filed in a near century of direct democracy in the state, and only fifty have qualified for the ballot.[6] By contrast, more than a hundred ballot initiatives a year are now filed with the state attorney general's office. This makes perverse sense. Why bother with a referendum (reversing a law of the legislature) or a recall of a legislator when an initiative permits you to write a law or constitutional amendment that the legislature will never be able to change on its own?

Such an inflexible system has many consequences. Budget priorities can be locked in easily, and they persist even when revenues diminish or when the priorities of a majority of Californians change. Civil rights may be taken away by the slimmest of majorities in the California system, while revising those restrictions often requires legislative supermajorities. Effectively, voters can set in cement laws and constitutional amendments that will govern the state long after they are dead or have moved away, even if new majorities would like something different.

Such a direct democracy isn't worthy of the name. It isn't very direct. And it surely isn't democratic. Put simply, initiatives provide voters not with direct engagement with their government, but with a way to circumvent their state government and frustrate future majorities.

MANY IDEAS DON'T ADDRESS
THE LEGISLATIVE DIVIDE

Since the 1911 special election that gave California its strange direct democracy, reformers have been trying to fix its defects. There is no shortage of ideas.

Restrictions on the process. Since 1920, when the legislature tried and failed to eliminate the initiative and referendum, state elites have been trying to impose limits on initiatives. Some reforms would limit the issues subject to initiative. Others would raise the number of signatures required to qualify an initiative.

Removing money from the process. In California, good-government groups have sought to impose limits on donations to initiative campaigns. They also have sought to ban or put restrictions on paid petition circulators, who do the overwhelming majority of signature gathering on initiative petitions.

Open up the process. Among the suggestions are to eliminate time limits for signature gathering, thus giving volunteer petition circulators more flexibility to collect the hundreds of thousands of signatures required for the ballot. In recent years, there have been efforts to permit signature gathering and petition circulation over the Internet.

Providing better information. A 2002 state commission and a more recent report by the Center for Governmental Studies each recommended upgrades to the information the state provides to voters about initiatives. CGS urged that restrictions be adopted on the lengths of measures—roughly a third of initiatives in the decade since 2000 have been more than 5,000 words, too long and too confusing for many voters.[7]

Each of these approaches, particularly those requiring more information for voters, has merit and might improve the process slightly. But all of them have drawbacks. Imposing new restrictions on the process could add to the costs of qualifying measures and running campaigns, thus making the initiative process even more of a rich person's game.

Many of the ideas for removing money from the process have been tried and struck down by federal and state courts as unconstitutional restrictions on political expression. On the other side, opening up the process and making the sponsorship of initiatives cheaper might produce more initiatives—and in California's system, that would mean more whips and chains that restrict the ability of elected leaders to govern effectively.

The big problem with these reforms is more fundamental. None of them address the divide in California's legislative branch, the inflexibility of the initiative process, and the problems of accountability that result.

Reckoning with these structural challenges requires a full redesign not only of the initiative process but also of the relationship between the legislature and direct democracy. Lawmakers and voters are now at odds, with each half of the legislative branch frustrated and hamstrung by the other. That divide must be bridged, so that the legislature better serves direct democracy, and direct democracy better serves the legislature.

SIX IDEAS FOR BRINGING VOTERS AND LAWMAKERS TOGETHER

Legislative reform and initiative reform can't be considered separately. They are two sides of the same coin. Lawmakers and voters should be partners in lawmaking—not antagonists who are free to work around each other. This requires two related sets of reforms. Not only must the initiative system be redesigned to bring the legislature into the process, as many commentators suggest. The legislature must also be changed to bring the voters into the process.

Successful reform in this area should not restrict voters or lawmakers. It should seek to free them, and give them more power and discretion— but in ways that allow them to engage in constructive conversation with each other.

The goal is nothing less than a more direct and more democratic direct democracy. Lawmakers must have more ability to balance priorities, budget, and legislate as best they see fit. This would be much more direct and democratic in an election system that, like the system suggested in Chapter 7, produces a legislature more representative of the state. At the same time, voters need to have greater freedom to pass judgment on the products of this greater legislative freedom.

Ideally, the two sides of the legislative branch would be integrated in a way that allows the legislature and voters to do what they do best. The legislature, using its time and staff and expertise, should have the unquestioned authority to legislate. Voters must have unquestioned authority to check the legislature, sending back laws and budgets they do not like for more work.

Fashioning reform requires reckoning with a hard political fact. Any new limits on the initiative process are poisonous. Yes, surveys show widespread public dissatisfaction with aspects of the process. But surveys also show that more than three in four California voters support retaining it. So scrapping direct democracy entirely is not a politically viable option. Nor should it be. A well-designed system of initiative and referendum would provide a useful check on representative government.

What would such a system look like? In essence, the legislative process and the direct democratic tools would be closely integrated, and as a result would more closely resemble each other. This would require six changes.

Require initiatives, as proposed laws and constitutional amendments, to adhere to the same rules as legislation. Initiative proponents would submit their language to nonpartisan staffers inside the capitol—at the legislative counsel's office, which would produce the actual legislative language of any measure that circulates. This would help prevent drafting errors and unintended consequences and produce clearer initiatives.

Most important, initiatives would no longer be immune from legislative amendment. Any initiative that passes would be subject to amendment or elimination by the legislature. There should no longer be two classes of laws—one passed by the legislature and subject to amendment, one passed by the voters and essentially protected from amendment.

Such a change would put California in line with its neighbors. Every other state permits legislative changes to initiatives, through either a majority vote, a supermajority vote, or a majority vote after a waiting period. Since supermajority votes, as we have seen repeatedly, are often antithetical to the goals of democratic accountability, a majority-vote rule for amending initiative statutes would be most effective. As a compromise, lawmakers might be required to wait for one legislative session (two years) after an initiative passes, out of respect for the will of the voters.

This would not be a radical change. Responsible initiative sponsors in California have often included provisions permitting the legislature to make amendments. Thirty-three of the forty-two initiatives approved by voters between 1990 and 2006 included some provision permitting legislative change. And Proposition 9, the 1974 Political Reform Act, which was one of the first initiatives to include language permitting legislative amendment without a vote of the people, has been amended more than two hundred times.[8]

Establish higher standards for constitutional amendments that give voters and lawmakers complementary powers to add to or subtract from the document. Currently, an amendment may be added with a simple majority vote of the people. But the constitution cannot be amended by the legislature, or substantially revised, without a two-thirds vote and another vote of the people. This dynamic—making it harder to edit or revise the document than it is to add to it—is one reason why California's constitution has grown so long.

Too many items better handled by statute, from taxes to the regulation of gill nets, find their way into the California constitution. To reverse that trend, new rules should make it more difficult to add to the constitution, and easier to revise it or edit things out. Voters and lawmakers should have similar powers in this area, and we propose two tracks.

The first track would permit the constitution to be amended or revised by a majority vote of the people—or a majority vote of the legislature, followed by a vote of the people—but only if the proposal showed sustained support over two election cycles. In the case of an amendment or revision offered via initiative, the proposed change would have to win a majority vote in two consecutive elections. If the legislature is the body introducing the change, the amendment or revision would have to win majority votes in two consecutive legislative sessions, with the people also approving by majority vote.

If faster constitutional action is required, a second track would permit quick passage but with a higher voting standard. To alter the constitution in just one cycle, two-thirds of voters would have to approve in the case of the initiative, or two-thirds of the legislature (followed by a vote of the people) if lawmakers offer the change.

To ensure that incremental reforms do not, over time, cripple the governing system, California should give voters and lawmakers additional power to "clean up" the document every decade. Once every twenty years, lawmakers would have to vote on whether to call a constitutional revision commission; if the body were approved, its recommendations would go to voters. And every other twenty years, voters would be asked directly if they would like to call a constitutional convention. Providing periodic, top-to-bottom constitutional review is common in other states. Since 1945, constitutional conventions have been held in Alaska, Connecticut, Georgia, Hawaii, Illinois, Louisiana, Michigan, Missouri, Montana, and Rhode Island. And the idea has been raised before in California. The 1878–79 convention debated an amendment that would have required a state constitutional convention every twenty-five years, beginning in 1903.[9]

Require any initiative that would impose supermajority voting rules to win the same supermajority of votes to become law.. For example, if a measure were to require a 55 percent vote of the legislature to raise taxes, the measure itself would have to receive 55 percent support at the polls. This would be an important check on supermajorities; Prop 13, which included the current two-thirds requirement for tax increases, was approved with a big majority but with less than two-thirds of the vote.

Require all ballot initiatives and bond measures to live within the legislative budget. To control the epidemic of something for nothing, every spending measure placed before voters needs to pay for itself, either with new revenue or with offsetting spending cuts.

This is already familiar territory in California. Local general obligation bonds approved by voters in school districts come with a built-in increase in the local property tax to repay the borrowed money, with interest. State bond measures also ought to be self-financing.

There are several ways to do that. For some kinds of infrastructure bonds, it would be best to simply return to the proven and economically sound principle of "user pay." The $20 billion transportation bond approved in 2006 could have been funded, for instance, with a 7 cent increase in the fuel tax. The 2006 flood control bond could have been at least partially paid for by fees on the property owners and water users who will benefit from the projects it will fund.

For bonds that fund projects that benefit all of us, the costs can be covered with a small increase in a general tax. For example, the state school bond approved in 2006 would have required an offsetting property tax increase of about $80 a year for a median-priced house in California.

Requiring bonds to be self-financing would have three major benefits. First, it would remove any mystery for voters about how bonds are paid for. The reality is, as Milton Friedman always reminded us, that to spend is to tax, something that is just as true when we are spending borrowed dollars. Second, self-financing would help correct the state's long-term structural deficit. Third, it would save taxpayers money, since state bonds can carry a lower interest rate when they have a dedicated tax source of repayment.

The same kind of pay-as-you-go requirement should also apply to initiative measures. Under this requirement, initiative sponsors who wish to increase state spending for a particular project—whether lengthening sentences on certain crimes or subsidizing purchases of natural gas–fueled vehicles—would have to include funding sufficient to pay for it, either by raising taxes and fees or by eliminating or reducing spending for some existing programs. In passing Proposition 58 in 2004, voters required that the budget enacted by the legislature and governor be balanced. There is no good reason voters should not impose the same discipline on themselves.

Permit the legislature to enact each initiative or place a counterproposal next to the initiative on the ballot. Under the current system, the legislature holds hearings on each initiative, but there is no formal mechanism for negotiations between initiative sponsors and lawmakers. There should be. Sponsors who qualify an initiative for the ballot should be guaranteed an up or down vote on the measure. In addition, lawmakers should be able to offer amendments that the initiative sponsor may accept or reject.

If the initiative sponsor rejects the legislature's amendments and decides to place the measure on the ballot anyway, the legislature should have the right to place a counterproposal on the ballot, on the same page as the initiative, via majority vote. Currently, a measure that is meant to counter a specific initiative may appear on the ballot, but not on the same page. As a result, it is often unclear to voters that they are reckoning with two competing proposals, one from the legislature and the other from an initiative sponsor.

Many countries that permit citizens' initiatives offer legislative counterproposals. Switzerland, which inspired California's direct democracy, permits legislative bodies to offer a counterproposal for every initiative. Sometimes, the counterproposal is constructive and seeks to meet the sponsor's goal by a different method. Sometimes, the counterproposal is a harsh rebuttal by the legislature. Whatever the case, Swiss ballots place a third question next to the initiative and the counterproposal: If both measures were to win, which would you prefer? This third questions offers two benefits. It permits voters who support the goal of both the initiative and the counterproposal to express a preference. And it allows voters who oppose a concept to choose the measure that they see as less threatening. (For a sample ballot, see Figure 6.)

California should adopt this three-question setup—initiative, counterproposal, and preference between the two—not only because it gives lawmakers more influence but also because it gives voters considerably more choice and power. Under the current system, voters have a simple binary choice on initiatives: yes or no. Under the three-question system, voters have eight voting options on each initiative, instead of just the two permitted under the current system. Consider:

1. Yes on initiative; yes on counterproposal; prefer initiative if both pass
2. Yes on initiative; yes on counterproposal; prefer counterproposal if both pass
3. Yes on initiative; no on counterproposal; prefer initiative if both pass

PROPOSITION 10A

○ Yes

○ No

TAX ON CIGARETTES. INITIATIVE CONSTITUTIONAL AMENDMENT AND STATUTE.

Imposes additional 13 cent tax on each cigarette distributed ($2.60 per pack), and indirectly increases tax on other tobacco products. Provides funding to qualified hospitals for emergency services, nursing education and health insurance to eligible children. Revenue also allocated to specified purposes including tobacco-use-prevention programs, enforcement of tobacco-related laws, and research, prevention, and treatment of various conditions. Increase in new state tobacco excise tax revenues of about $2.1 billion annually by 2011-12, declining slightly annually thereafter. Those revenues would be spent for various health programs, children's health coverage, and tobacco-related programs.

PROPOSITION 10B

○ Yes

○ No

TAX ON CIGARETTES. LEGISLATIVE STATUTE. COUNTERPROPOSAL.

Imposes additional 13 cent tax on each cigarette distributed ($2.60 per pack), and indirectly increases tax on other tobacco products. Allocates revenue to General Fund. Increase in new state tobacco excise tax revenues of about $2.1 billion annually by 2011–12, declining slightly annually thereafter.

PROPOSITION 10C

○ 10A

○ 10B

WHICH MEASURE DO YOU WISH TO BECOME LAW IF BOTH PROPOSITION 10A, THE VOTER INITIATIVE, AND PROPOSITION 10B, THE LEGISLATIVE COUNTERPROPOSAL, RECEIVE A MAJORITY OF VOTES?

Figure 6   Sample Ballot: Initiative, Counterproposal, and Voter Preference

4. Yes on initiative; no on counterproposal; prefer counterproposal (an unlikely and irrational preference, obviously)
5. No on initiative; yes on counterproposal; prefer initiative (also unlikely)
6. No on initiative; yes on counterproposal; prefer counterproposal if both pass
7. No on initiative; no on counterproposal; prefer initiative if both pass
8. No on initiative; no on counterproposal; prefer counterproposal if both pass

In a three-question initiative system, campaigns would produce more-informed voters. How? Under the current system, voters must consider an initiative in isolation, without any point of comparison. Emotions about the issue often drive debate, and the details of the specific measure get little scrutiny. But in a three-question system, a campaign is likely to be comparative, focusing attention and debate on the contents of the two measures. The central question of such a race would be: what are the differences between these two measures? Such comparative campaigns would produce scrutiny of the legislative details and help voters make more-informed choices. Information is power.

Make it easier for voters to overturn the legislature through a more referendum-based direct democracy. Reform to the initiative process must enhance lawmakers' power by ensuring that the legislature is the undisputed headquarters of writing and drafting new laws. By retaining the power to amend initiatives, legislators would find no part of the law off-limits.

But in such a revamped system, voters would need additional power to check the legislature. That power could be found in an oft-neglected tool of California's direct democracy: the referendum.

A referendum is a ballot measure that does not propose a law—but instead permits voters to block an act of the legislature. The California state constitution, as we have seen, is biased in favor of the initiative. It is just as easy to get enough signatures to qualify an initiative as it is to qualify a referendum. And it is usually less expensive to qualify an initiative, because the time limit for doing so is two months longer than the ninety-day limit for a referendum. Signature gatherers can charge ballot measure sponsors more money for their work when they know time is short.

In addition, the constitution makes it possible for initiatives to be introduced on almost any subject matter. The referendum power, however, is limited to certain legislative subjects and to measures passed in the normal course of business. Tax and appropriation bills and legislation passed under "urgency," or emergency, provisions are exempt from referendum. As a result, fewer than seventy-five referendums were filed for the ballot in California in the century since 1911. Over the same period, more than 1,100 initiatives were filed and more than 300 qualified for the ballot. This initiative-centered direct democracy is unique to California and other western states. In the rest of the world, the referendum, or reversal of legislative action, not the initiative, is by far the most common type of ballot measure.

To balance the enhanced power of lawmakers to amend initiatives, voters need more power to block them via referendum. This could be accomplished in several ways. The signature-gathering standards for a referendum might be lowered substantially, perhaps to 1 percent of the number of votes cast in the most recent gubernatorial election. With such a standard, enough signatures to qualify a referendum could be gathered in a matter of weeks. Under a system that provides for quick referendums, urgency and some tax and spending bills could be made subject to voter reversals as well.

Such a reform would not reduce the number of ballot measures or the ability of the people to decide big questions. If anything, it might give people more measures and more choices. But the goal would be to make most California ballot measures referendums—verdicts on the product of the legislature—instead of initiatives.

When Californians vote on initiatives, they are voting on proposed laws and amendments that have not been vetted in the legislature. This may be democracy, but it is not a direct judgment on the government. It is an end run around that government. A referendum-based system, by its very nature, would be more integrated with the legislative process. When they vote on referendums, they are passing judgment on the legislature. That is direct communication between the people and their elected officials.

How might such a system work in practice? Ideally, lawmakers and voters would be partners, with the legislature making suggestions and the public saying yea or nay. It is likely that controversial legislation would be presented to the people multiple times before winning approval. (In Switzerland, repeated referendums on major legislation are central to the political culture.) This process would not be without rancor. But it would channel the rancor into democratic verdicts, as voters and lawmakers bat proposals back and forth until majorities of legislators and voters agree.

DIRECT DEMOCRACY
WITH ACCOUNTABILITY

This system would offer more power and choice to voters. It also would provide more power and autonomy for elected representatives in legislation. And there would be more direct interplay between voters and legislators, via counterproposals and more frequent referendums.

Legislators would be more accountable for their work, since, under a referendum-based system, they frequently would have to convince voters to accept their deals and compromises. Much of the money and scrutiny that initiatives currently attract would be redirected to the legislature, the source of referendums upon which voters would pass judgment. Voters would have to pay more attention to the legislature; they would be voting not on initiative abstractions but on legislative deals, with all their trade-offs.

With these reforms, California's system of initiative and referendum would be worthy of the name "direct democracy."

EPILOGUE
GOOD RULES
TO MATCH ITS MOUNTAINS

In 2009, the Pew Center on the States surveyed forty-nine states with this question in mind: how closely did their governing systems and economic challenges resemble those of California? It went without saying that any resemblance to California was a sure sign of peril. "California's problems are in a league of their own," the Pew study said in its introduction. "But the same pressures that drove it toward fiscal disaster are wreaking havoc in a number of states, with potentially damaging consequences for the entire country."[1]

California is America writ early. Its civic diseases cross the Sierra Nevada or the Colorado River as easily as its blockbusters, gadgets, and cabernet. California's troubles, in fact, may hint at a coming crisis in American states. After all, if the extraterrestrial Tocqueville who visited California in Chapter 1 were to beam down into many other state capitols, he would find similar clashes between the three contradictory systems: majority-producing elections (based on single-member, geography-based districts), budget systems that require supermajorities or other forms of consensus, and majoritarian direct democracy. It is California's misfortune to have the most dysfunctional combination of these systems. But it is hardly the only state whose citizens must live with these contradictions.

Symptoms of the California disease are most visible in its closest neighbors. In Arizona, lawmakers routinely pretend to balance budgets with California-style accounting gimmicks and questionable borrowing because they are, as Pew noted, "hamstrung by voter-imposed spending constraints, a tax structure highly reliant on a growing economy, and a series of tax cuts, made in the 1990s, that has limited revenue." Nevada's tax system is a mess and resists changes "because, unlike most states" (but like California), "Nevada has written some of its tax laws into the constitution." In Oregon, a voter-approved cap on revenue "forces the state to deliver rebates to taxpayers when times are good but . . . can strip it of much-needed revenue when times are bad."[2]

The Pew survey identified nine states—Arizona, Florida, Illinois, Michigan, Nevada, New Jersey, Oregon, Rhode Island, and Wisconsin—that resembled California in their governing and fiscal dysfunction, particularly in erecting "legal obstacles to balanced budgets." Six of these states, it is worth noting, had adopted some form of the supermajority restrictions on taxation, spending, and other policy decisions that have made California so difficult to govern. Pew put five more states—Colorado, Georgia, Hawaii, Kentucky, and New York—on a watch list because they were trending in the direction of Golden State dysfunction.

"What we may be seeing is America starting to be Californiafied," the Nobel Prize–winning economist Paul Krugman wrote in the *New York Times*.[3]

California has a choice: wait for contagion to make its own dysfunction seem less abnormal; or do what Californians, in their economic and social lives, do best—design the new, and show America the future.

A NEW, INTEGRATED SYSTEM

The proposals we have outlined in this book are not random reforms. They are meant to work together to create something new: a more democratic operating system for California. Many of our specific proposals are not themselves novel. In fact, most are ideas and practices well tested and proven to work in other states and countries. Our California fix uses the method that shapes so much of California life, from its cooking to its architecture to its iPhones. It pulls together the best from all over to create a new integrated system, one designed to be more democratic, accountable, and flexible.

It starts by junking the current election system, which produces a polarized legislature that is neither fully representative nor accountable to voters. In its place goes a more representative legislature, its members closer to the voters and elected via multimember districts and proportional representation so that the vote of every Californian may be said to count.

Creating a fully representative and accountable legislature permits a second change: the end of the system of fiscal whips and chains, in which supermajority vote requirements are clamped on lawmakers because the public does not trust them. Policy choices on taxes and spending would be removed from the constitution. Fiscal discipline would be established through commonsense practices, such as honest accounting and pay-as-you-go budgeting, and enforced by voters at elections in which control of the legislature would always be a live political issue. The new operating system would further advance accountability and fiscal responsibility by realigning state and local governments so that more of the decisions about funding programs and running them are made by the same people, at the same level of government, often closer to the voters.

The third big piece of the California fix re-imagines our inflexible, initiative-heavy system of direct democracy as a referendum-centered system in which lawmakers and voters are more accountable to each other. Elected officials should have more authority over the drafting and amending of legislation, while those voters and interests who wished to use the ballot would have greater authority to use the referendum to intervene directly on the legislation that Sacramento produces.

Each reform would build on the others. More democratic and representative election processes would make it easier to hold lawmakers accountable and reshape the legislature. In turn, these lawmakers would have more freedom to reshape the law with the times and hold powerful interests at bay. And finally, the people, via new and more forceful powers of referendum, would be able to reshape the legislative product of these legislators.

This is a lift heavier than even the most steroid-addled strongman might attempt. We know that these proposals push the boundaries of the politically possible. But in California, almost every proposal pushes those boundaries. Even modest reforms that will do little to fix the state's structural problems—ending the supermajority requirement to pass a budget; the jungle primary; changes in signature-gathering standards for initiatives—receive less than majority support in polls.

Far too often, the skepticism of California voters, their hearts hardened by round after round of failed incremental reform, has been used as an excuse not to think big. We understand this kind of pragmatism. As a group, California voters are not unlike the worst boyfriend or girlfriend you've ever had. The electorate—thoroughly devoted to something-for-nothing, low-tax, high-spending politics—believes its needs can be met with little cost or effort. The electorate is angry and frustrated at the status quo. But the electorate can't tell you what they would like you to do to make them happier.

When small changes in California's system are so politically difficult, the economic principle of opportunity costs suggests targeting our energy and attention on the bigger, systemic changes that would fix the problem. Or to put it another way, when defeat is likely, why not try what works?

We fear that proposals offered by California Forward, one of the two leading reform efforts, fail the efficacy test. Organized by leading foundations, California Forward is led, staffed, and advised by political insiders who are themselves authors of today's dysfunctional system. When they produced specific initiatives for addressing the state's problems in 2009, the recommendations were narrowly tailored to give no offense to major interest groups. One proposal seeks to change the budget process—by requiring more long-term planning, more reviews of programs, more rules for paying off debt and funding new programs, and more supermajority votes on revenues from fees. Another would grant local governments more control over local money—and more authority to cooperate with each other—but would mandate how much of any new revenues must be distributed.

But these ideas offer little to alter the three-headed system of contradictions that the extraterrestrial Tocqueville would have confronted—with majoritarian elections for a polarized polity, a consensus-based supermajority system for making decisions on the polarizing issue of taxes and spending, and the majoritarian initiative process that sought to overrule that consensus system. In seeking to reform without changing the structure, California Forward would embed the contradictions further into the state system. In this approach, there is more than a little of what sociologist C. Wright Mills called "crackpot realism."[4]

The Bay Area Council's constitutional convention proposals, which stalled in early 2010 for lack of financial support, raised the opposite concern—of overreaching. Although constitutional conventions have a long and honored history in America, the idea of actually calling one makes many people nervous. They invest it with their worst fears: that their neighbors, gathered in convention, will repeal fundamental rights or raid their pocketbooks. The Bay Area Council proposal compounded this worry by shifting the selection of convention delegates out of the hands of voters—the constitution provides for election of delegates by Assembly districts—and into a hybrid system in which delegates would be selected partly at random and partly by local officials.

A constitutional convention has built-in risks. Voters, after all, might not call the convention. And, if called, a convention might not produce a coherent new governing system. But by trying to take the politics out of what must inevitably be a political process, the Bay Area Council made a third risk even greater. Even in the event of twin miracles—a convention is called and passes a solid plan—voters would have to ratify all changes in the face of almost certain opposition from the ideological and interest groups that the process has deliberately excluded from the deliberations. Only a constitutional convention, or a constitutional revision enacted by the legislature, can produce the scope of governance reform we believe is necessary. But it is unlikely to be delivered by any method that denies the reality of political differences or ignores the need for a bargain to be struck by California's contending forces.

The state's current stalemate, while a formidable obstacle, is no more formidable than that faced by those who framed the state's constitution in the nineteenth century, or than that confronted by the Progressives a century ago, when they elected a governor in the face of opposition from both parties and the railroad. And the changes we propose are far less radical than the Progressives' push for direct democracy, which represented a sharp break with American history and its Madisonian system of divided government, checks and balances, and suspicion of democracy.

The fall of 2011 will mark the centennial of the 1911 special election in which the Progressives remade the state government's operating system.

It is long past time for an update.

WHEN THE GOLD RUNS OUT

Behind every new governing system lies a political deal, clinched with a handshake. Our proposed California fix can't happen until both the left and the right of California politics agree that the schizophrenic system we have now keeps them from achieving what they want. The left and the right each hold hostages in our current system. The left enjoys the Proposition 98 school-funding guarantee, a host of voter-approved spending programs, and the backing of public employee unions that benefit from the centralization of government. The right enjoys the leverage provided by Proposition 13 and the two-thirds vote on appropriations and taxation. To fix the system, both sides must give up these hostages.

In these times of endless political rancor, that is a long shot. But that reality doesn't change another reality: the hostages must be surrendered before California can devise a system that works.

Something else must be surrendered too: the relentless scapegoating of individuals for California's troubles. This scapegoating is a by-product of a dangerous but dominant idea in California politics: that there is nothing wrong with California's governing structure; people are at fault.

There are two versions of this argument. The version that dominates public opinion might be called the Rodney King fallacy, after his plea during the 1992 Los Angeles riots: "I just want to say, can we all get along?" This version says that the state's system would work if we had better people in elected offices who were more inclined to work together. The second version, which dominates among the state's political elite, is that the system would work better if the people weren't so silly or selfish or stupid—that California would be a paradise again if we had better Californians.

Neither version explains the California crackup. The singular nature of the state's present fix is that, at the same time, everyone is to blame and no one is to blame.

There's no evidence that lawmakers in Sacramento are less public-spirited than their predecessors or counterparts around the country. They have been reduced to being a cleanup crew for a rotten governing system because that is the job the system assigns them.

Nor is there any reason to believe that Californians are more susceptible than other Americans to the vices of wanting quick fixes and something for nothing. The California electorate could be flooded with the most civic-minded of citizens, people reared and schooled in the commonsense progressive traditions of places such as Iowa and Minnesota, with little change in the levels of frustration. We know this because it's what has happened in California over the past six decades. They came, they voted, and now they wonder what went wrong.

"MATCH MY MOUNTAINS"

Writing six decades ago, at the end of California's first century, Carey McWilliams suggested that one day the state's growth and talented arrivals and natural advantages would no longer be enough to ensure success. "California needs men who can see beyond its mountains, men who can see the entire West and who realize that, as with all good things, there comes a time when the gold runs out, when the exception disappears in the rule," he wrote.[5]

McWilliams, borrowing a line from the poet Yeats about the "brute blood of air,"[6] hoped that California would end its all-consuming political fights: "California 'being so caught up, so mastered by the brute blood of the air' must, indeed, put on knowledge with its power and adopt, as an official policy, the same generous open-handedness with which its magic mountains have showered benefits on those lucky people, the Californians."

An open hand. There could be no better symbol of the transformation California needs—the unclenching of a fist.

The scroll at the state capitol in Sacramento reads: "Bring Me Men to Match My Mountains!" California already has such men and women. What the state requires, and has never had, are rules, good rules, clear and limited, and yet grand enough to match its mountains and to meet its future.

NOTES

PROLOGUE. OUT OF LUCK

1. Josiah Royce, *California* (Santa Barbara: Peregrine Publishers, 1970), 3.
2. Jerry Roberts and Phil Trounstine, "California's Uninspiring Candidates for Governor," *Los Angeles Times*, November 3, 2009.
3. Carey McWilliams, *California: The Great Exception* (Berkeley: University of California Press, 1949).
4. Peter Schrag, *Paradise Lost: California's Experience, America's Future* (Berkeley: University of California Press, 1998).
5. Jack Rakove, *Original Meanings: Politics and Ideas in the Making of the Constitution* (New York: Knopf, 1996), 23–56.
6. Quoted in ibid., 36.

1. CRISIS WITHOUT EXIT

1. Gale Kaufman, interview with the authors, October 15, 2009.
2. Phil Isenberg, interview with the authors, October 14, 2009.
3. Population figures are from Department of Finance data and estimates, http://www.ca.gov/About/Facts/Population.html_4.
4. *Record Union* (Sacramento), June 17, 1878, quoted in William Deverell,

Railroad Crossing: Californians and the Railroad, 1850–1910 (Berkeley: University of California Press, 1994), 47.

5. Phillip Reese, "Golden State Losing Folks as Old Dust Bowl Beckons," *Sacramento Bee*, June 14, 2009, 1A.

6. Henry George, "What the Railroad Will Bring Us," *Overland Monthly* 1, no. 4 (October 1868).

7. Quoted in James N. Gregory, *American Exodus: The Dust Bowl Migration and Okie Culture in California* (New York: Oxford University Press, 1989), 80, 96.

8. Dowell Myers, John Pitkin, and Ricardo Ramirez, *The New Homegrown Majority in California* (Los Angeles: University of Southern California, School of Policy Planning and Development, April 2009), 4 and appendix A.

9. D'Vera Cohn, "Magnet or Sticky? A State by State Typology," March 11, 2009, Pew Research Center, http://pewresearch.org/pubs/1146/magnet-sticky -states-typology, accessed November 6, 2009.

10. Myers, Pitkin, and Ramirez, *Homegrown Majority*, 5–6.

11. Ibid., 11.

12. Ibid.

13. Timm Herdt, "$16 Million Initiative Aims to Promote Reform in the State," *Ventura County Star*, March 27, 2008.

2. HISTORY AND THE CONSTITUTION

1. E. B. Willis and P. K. Stockton, *Debates and Proceedings of the Constitutional Convention*, vol. 3 (Sacramento: State Printing Office, 1880), 1525–26.

2. Carey McWilliams, *California: The Great Exception* (Berkeley: University of California Press, 1949), 17.

3. McWilliams, *California*, 42.

4. John Ross Browne, *Report of the Debates in the Convention of California* (Washington, D.C.: J. T. Towers, 1850), 24.

5. Ibid., 418–61. Original handwritten notes of the convention, on file at the Bancroft Library at the University of California, Berkeley.

6. Convention notes, on file at the Bancroft Library.

7. Hinton Helper, *The Land of Gold* (1855), http://books.google.com/books ?id=h4MUAAAAYAAJ&dq=land%20of%20gold&pg=PR1#v=onepage&q= &f=false.

8. Willis and Stockton, *Debates and Proceedings*, vol. 1, 18.

9. Ibid., vol. 2, 923.

10. Ibid., vol. 1, 59.

11. Ibid., 149.

12. George Mowry, *The California Progressives* (New York: Times Books, 1963), 99.

13. Letter from Hiram Johnson to Fremont Older, March 14, 1913, Hiram Johnson Papers, Bancroft Library, University of California, Berkeley. Johnson wrote of himself and his wife, whom he referred to as "the Boss": "I fear that neither of us temperamentally is fitted for official position. I because I take things too seriously and permit small matters to distress me unduly, and the Boss because naturally position and power, publicity and limelight, are repugnant to her."

14. "Johnson at Dreamland Rink," *San Francisco Examiner*, June 8, 1910, 1.

15. Hiram Johnson, speech at Armory Hall in Sacramento, October 16, 1914, Johnson Papers.

16. Letter from Hiram Johnson to Chester Rowell, September 15, 1915, Johnson Papers.

17. Tony Quinn, "Origins of a Stalemate," *California Journal of Politics and Policy* 1, no. 1, Article 7, http://www.bepress.com/cjpp/vol1/iss1/7/.

18. V. O. Key and Winston Crouch, *The Initiative and Referendum in California* (Berkeley: University of California Press, 1939), 487.

19. McWilliams, *California*, 180.

20. Hiram Johnson, Palm Springs speech, May 25, 1910, Johnson papers.

21. McWilliams, *California*, 19.

22. J. Gould, "Report on Materials of Constitution Revision Commission Relating to Provisions in California Constitution Recommended or Endorsed by Commission," December 10, 1974, 1.

23. Barry Keene, remarks, Matsui Center panel on constitutional reform, Sacramento, October 14, 2009.

24. Gould, "Report on Materials of Constitution Revision Commission," 11.

25. Dwayne Hunn and Doris Ober, *Ordinary People Doing the Extraordinary: The Story of Ed and Joyce Koupal and the Initiative Process* (Los Angeles: The People's Lobby, 2001).

3. EMPOWERING AND
SHACKLING SACRAMENTO

1. Doug Shuit, "Property Taxes: Increases Cut Deep into Budgets," *Los Angeles Times*, August 1, 1976, B1.

2. Clarence Y. H. Lo, *Small Property versus Big Government: Social Origins of the Property Tax Revolt* (Berkeley: University of California Press, 1995), 55; Frank Levy, "On Understanding Proposition 13," *Public Interest*, no. 56 (Summer 1979): 74.

3. Isaac William Martin, *The Permanent Tax Revolt: How the Property Tax Transformed American Politics* (Stanford, Calif.: Stanford University Press, 2008), 38–42, 44–46; David R. Doerr, *California's Tax Machine: A History of Taxing and Spending in the Golden State* (Sacramento: California Taxpayers' Association, 2000), 69–79.

4. Lo, *Small Property*, 8.

5. Levy, "On Understanding Proposition 13," 69; Lo, *Small Property*, 70–111; Richard Nevins, interview by Jackson K. Putnam and Lawrence B. de Graaf, 1987 and 1989, transcript, State Government Oral History Program, California State Archives, Sacramento, 140, 186–92, 228.

6. Similar reforms of property tax administration in other states also produced homeowner protest movements. See Martin, *Permanent Tax Revolt*, 61–95; Robert Kuttner, *Revolt of the Haves: Tax Rebellions and Hard Times* (New York: Simon and Schuster, 1980), 41–43.

7. Kuttner, *Revolt of the Haves*, 50–51.

8. Quoted in Lo, *Small Property*, 64.

9. Mike Davis, *City of Quartz* (New York: Vintage, 1992), 181.

10. Leo McCarthy, interview by Carole Hicke, Regional Oral History Office, University of California, Berkeley, 1995 and 1996, transcript, State Government Oral History Program, California State Archives, Sacramento, 126.

11. Quoted in Lo, *Small Property*, 162.

12. Peter Behr, interview by Ann Lage, Regional Oral History Office, University of California, Berkeley, 1988 and 1989, transcript, State Government Oral History Program, California State Archives, Sacramento, 324.

13. Bill Lockyer, interview with the authors, August 13, 2009.

14. Jerry Brown, interview with the authors, August 26, 2009.

15. Kuttner, *Revolt of the Haves*, 57–65; Doerr, *California's Tax Machine*, 133–37; Levy, "On Understanding Proposition 12," 81–84; McCarthy interview, 123.

16. Behr interview, 346.

17. David O. Sears and Jack Citrin, *Tax Revolt: Something for Nothing in California* (Cambridge, Mass.: Harvard University Press, 1985), 43–72.

18. Levy, "On Understanding Proposition 13," 67; Terry Schwadron and Paul Richter, *California and the American Tax Revolt: Proposition 13 Five Years Later* (Berkeley: University of California Press, 1984), 79.

19. McCarthy interview, 127.

20. Lockyer interview.

21. Schwadron and Richter, *California and the American Tax Revolt*, 24; Howard Jarvis with Robert Pack, *I'm Mad as Hell* (New York: Times Books, 1979), 295; Lockyer interview.

22. David Cay Johnston, *Free Lunch: How the Wealthiest Americans Enrich Themselves at Government Expense (and Stick You with the Bill)* (New York: Portfolio, 2007), 57–60.

23. Schwadron and Richter, *California and the American Tax Revolt*, 121–74. The authors' copy, purchased from a used-book seller, carries a sticker indicating it once sat on the shelf of an Orange County library branch that no longer exists.

24. Tony Quinn, "Origins of a Stalemate," *California Journal of Politics and Policy* 1, no. 1 (2009), http://www.bepress.com/cjpp/vol1/iss1/4.

25. Steve Wiegand, "Going Broke: Two-Thirds Rule on Budget Has Fans, Foes," *Sacramento Bee*, September 22, 2009.

26. Ken Maddy, interview by Donald B. Seney, 1999, transcript, State Government Oral History Program, California State Archives, Sacramento, 944.

27. Quoted in Schwadron and Richter, *California and the American Tax Revolt*, 101.

28. Behr interview, 350.

29. McCarthy interview, 130.

30. Behr interview, 350.

31. Kirk Stark and Jonathan Zasloff, "Tiebout and Tax Revolts: Did Serrano Really Cause Proposition 13?" *UCLA Law Review* 50 (2002–2003): 808–11; Jon Sonstelie, Eric Brunner, and Kenneth Ardon, *For Better or for Worse? School Finance Reform in California* (San Francisco: Public Policy Institute of California, 2000), 52–54.

32. Schwadron and Richter, *California and the American Tax Revolt*, 100.

33. California Secretary of State, *The Lobbying Directory, 2009–2010*, http://www.sos.ca.gov/prd/Lobbying_Directory.pdf; Shane Goldmacher, "Lobbyists Spend Millions—and Rarely Lose in Legislature," *Sacramento Bee*, March 29, 2009, 1A; Fair Political Practices Commission, *A Report on Lobbying: Payments to Influence Legislative and Administrative Action, 1977–78* (Sacramento: FPPC, 1979); Jim Sanders, "Local Government Lobbying Costs Soar in California," *Sacramento Bee*, February 9, 2009, 1A.

34. McCarthy interview, 130.

35. Gary Hart, interview with the authors, October 14, 2009.

36. Ibid.; Jason A. Grissom, *Who Sits on School Boards in California?* (Stanford, Calif.: Institute for Research on Education Policy and Practice, 2007), 7; Frederick M. Hess, *School Boards at the Dawn of the 21st Century* (Alexandria, Va.: National School Boards Association, 2002), 27.

37. Peter Schrag, *Paradise Lost: California's Experience, America's Future* (Berkeley: University of California Press, 1999), 75–78; Phillip Reese, "Metro Fire Has Big Paydays: Four-Fifths of Workers Earn More Than $100,000," *Sacramento Bee*, May 10, 2009, B1; Bureau of Labor Statistics, "County Employment and Wages in California: Fourth Quarter 2008," press release, BLS 09–84, September 10, 2009.

38. Hart interview.

4. FROM TEACHERS TO JANITORS: DIRECT DEMOCRACY DEMOTES THE LEGISLATURE

1. William K. "Sandy" Muir Jr., *Legislature: California's School for Politics* (Chicago: University of Chicago Press, 1982), 8.

2. Fernando Quintero, "From the Halls of Ivy to Halls of Government?" *The Berkeleyan*, March 6, 1996.

3. Muir, *Legislature*, 11.

4. William K. "Sandy" Muir Jr., interview with the authors, October 20, 2009.

5. Kenneth Howe, "Well-Paid Armies Wielding Clipboards," *San Francisco Chronicle*, May 19, 1998, A-1.

6. Fred Kimball, interview with Joe Mathews, June 2008, conducted for Joe Mathews, "Betting on the Lottery," *Los Angeles Times*, June 22, 2008, A-17.

7. Some California initiatives include language permitting them to be altered by the legislature. Unless such specific authorization of legislative action is included in the initiative language, an initiative statute cannot be altered by the legislature without another vote of the people.

8. John Mockler, interview with Joe Mathews, October 17, 2004, conducted for Joe Mathews, *The People's Machine* (New York: PublicAffairs Books, 2006).

9. John Mockler, interview with Joe Mathews, April 1, 2008; also from Joe Mathews, "The Mystery of Prop 98," *Los Angeles Times*, July 13, 2008, Sunday Opinion, 1.

10. John van de Kamp, telephone interview with Joe Mathews, November 9, 2003, quoted in Joe Mathews, "Schwarzenegger's Populist Beliefs Guide His Strategy," *Los Angeles Times*, November 24, 2003, A1.

11. Pete Wilson, interview with Joe Mathews, February 22, 2005. Wilson says he felt a personal revulsion to crime. While working as a young cop in Chicago, his grandfather, an Irish immigrant, had been gunned down by a member of a gang engaged in the theft and selling of cocaine.

12. George Gorton, interview with Joe Mathews, June 21, 2004. Also quoted in Mathews, *The People's Machine*, 20.

13. One of this book's authors, Mark Paul, was the Treasurer's Office employee who received the phone call.

14. State Treasurer's Office, *Looking beyond the Horizon: Investment Planning for the 21st Century* (Sacramento: October 2007).

15. Muir, *Legislature*, 81–82.

16. Eugene C. Lee, "The Initiative Boom: An Excess of Democracy," *Governing California: Politics, Government, and Public Policy in the Golden State* (Berkeley: Institute of Governmental Studies Press, 2006), 140–41.

17. Muir, *Legislature*, 162.

18. Alfred E. Alquist, interview by Donald B. Seney, 1997, transcript, State Government Oral History Program, California State Archives, Sacramento, 160.

5. BUDGETING WITHOUT SHACKLES

1. For a fiscal review of the Deukmejian and Wilson years, see Daniel J. B. Mitchell, "From JerryRigged to Petered Out: Lessons from the Deukmejian Era for Contemporary California State Budgeting," in Daniel J. B. Mitchell, ed., *California Policy Options 2008* (Los Angeles: School of Public Policy and Social Research, University of California at Los Angeles, 2008), 39–76; and Daniel J. B. Mitchell, "Wilson's Woes Should Keep Us on Our Toes: Where Is Plan B for the California State Budget?" in Daniel J. B. Mitchell, ed., *California Policy Options 2007* (Los Angeles: School of Public Policy and Social Research, University of California at Los Angeles, 2007), 31–78.

2. National Governors Association and the National Association of State Budget Officers, *Fiscal Survey of the States* (Washington, D.C.: National Association of State Budget Officers, December 2009), 1; Eric McGhee, *At Issue: Legislative Reform* (San Francisco: Public Policy Institute of California, 2007), 4.

3. Bruce E. Cain and George A. Mackenzie, *Are California's Fiscal Constraints Institutional or Political?* (San Francisco: Public Policy Institute of California, 2008), 8–9.

4. George Raine, "Rivals Wrangle—Except One," *San Francisco Chronicle*,

September 4, 2003, A-1; Governor Arnold Schwarzenegger, *2008 State of the State Address*, January 8, 2008.

5. "Reactions to the May Budget," *Sacramento Bee*, Capitol Alert blog, May 14, 2008, http://www.sacbee.com/static/weblogs/capitolalertlatest/012576.html.

6. Mark DiCamillo and Mervin Field, "The Changing California Electorate (Part 2)" (San Francisco: Field Research Corporation, 2009); Mark Baldassare et al., *California Survey: Californians and the Environment* (San Francisco: Public Policy Institute of California, 2009).

7. Mark Paul, "California's Budget Mess," video, New America Foundation, April 27, 2009, http://www.youtube.com/watch?v=HH4dm6guSCE; State and Local Government Finance Data Query System, http://www.taxpolicycenter.org/slf-dqs/pages.cfm, Urban Institute-Brookings Institution Tax Policy Center, data from U.S. Census Bureau, *Annual Survey of State and Local Government Finances, Government Finances*, vol. 4, and *Census of Governments* (Years), accessed July 28, 2008.

8. For a summary of the research, see Cain and Mackenzie, *Fiscal Constraints*, 10.

9. McClintock quoted in George Skelton, "Allow a Majority Budget Vote at Last," *Los Angeles Times*, September 8, 2008.

10. Julie Tamaki and Miguel Bustillo, "Assembly Approves State Budget," *Los Angeles Times*, July 17, 2001, A-1; California Constitutional Revision Commission, *Final Report and Recommendations to the Governor and the Legislature* (Sacramento, 1996), 43.

11. Cain and Mackenzie, *Fiscal Constraints*, 10.

12. State and Local Government Finance Data Query System, http://www.taxpolicycenter.org/slf-dqs/pages.cfm; Mark Paul, "Riding the Ratchet," *American Interest* 5, no. 1 (September/October 2009): 116–20; California Budget Project, *Budget Brief: To Have and Have Not* (Sacramento: California Budget Project, June 2009).

13. California Secretary of State, *Official Voter Information Guide: Supplemental*, March 2004 primary election, 15; John Decker, "What Do Debt Loads Say about California's Fiscal Condition?" *California Journal of Politics and Policy* (Berkeley: Berkeley Electronic Press, 2009), http://www.bepress.com/cjpp/vol1/iss1/9; letter from Mac Taylor to Assemblyman Juan Arambula, July 30, 2009, http://www.lao.ca.gov/2009/bud/liabilities/CA_Liabilities_073009.pdf.

14. California Teachers Association, "School Funding," http://www.cta.org/issues/other/School+Funding.htm, accessed August 31, 2009; Jack O'Connell,

"State of Education Address 2009," February 3, 2009, http://www.cde.ca.gov/eo/ in/se/yro9stateofed.asp; Paula S. Campbell, "California School Funding: 'Worse Than a Retreat; It Is a Massacre,'" *California Progress Report* blog, June 1, 2009, http://www.californiaprogressreport.com/2009/06/california_scho_1.html.

15. Stephen J. Carroll et al., *California's K–12 Public Schools: How Are They Doing?* (Santa Monica: RAND Corporation, 2004), 43–46; Susanna Loeb, Jason Grissom, and Katharine Strunk, *District Dollars: Painting a Picture of Revenues and Expenditures in California's School Districts* (Stanford, Calif.: Institute for Research on Education Policy and Practice, March 2007), 5.

16. Carroll et al., *California's K–12 Public Schools*, iv–v; Heather Rose et al., *High Expectations, Modest Means: The Challenge Facing California's Public Schools* (San Francisco: Public Policy Institute of California, 2003), 50–53.

17. Robert Dahl, *How Democratic Is the American Constitution?* 2nd ed. (New Haven, Conn.: Yale University Press, 2003), 131.

18. James Madison, "Federalist LVIII," in *Madison: Writings* (New York: Library of America, 1999), 337.

19. Ibid., 337.

20. Evan Halper and Michael Rothfield, "A Tense Countdown to Passage of California's Budget," *Los Angeles Times*, February 21, 2009, A-1; *California Penal Code*, sec. 86. The provision reads: "86. Every Member of either house of the Legislature, or any member of the legislative body of a city, county, city and county, school district, or other special district, who asks for, receives, or agrees to receive, any bribe, upon any understanding that his or her official vote, opinion, judgment, or action shall be influenced thereby, *or shall give, in any particular manner, or upon any particular side of any question or matter upon which he or she may be required to act in his or her official capacity, or gives, or offers or promises to give, any official vote in consideration that another Member of the Legislature, or another member of the legislative body of a city, county, city and county, school district, or other special district shall give this vote either upon the same or another question,* is punishable by imprisonment in the state prison for two, three, or four years and, in cases in which no bribe has been actually received, by a restitution fine of not less than two thousand dollars ($2,000) or not more than ten thousand dollars ($10,000) or, in cases in which a bribe was actually received, by a restitution fine of at least the actual amount of the bribe received or two thousand dollars ($2,000), whichever is greater, or any larger amount of not more than double the amount of any bribe received or ten thousand dollars ($10,000), whichever is greater." (Italics added.)

21. Dahl, *How Democratic Is the American Constitution?* 164–67.

22. Werner Z. Hirsch and Daniel J. B. Mitchell, "Family Time, Cliffs, and Train Wrecks: Recalling California's State Budget" (January 1, 2004), UCLA School of Public Affairs, California Policy Options, Paper 921, http://repositories .cdlib.org/uclaspa/cpo/921.

23. Mark Paul, "Budget Confusion in California," *Los Angeles Times*, "Opinion," May 7, 2008; Hirsch and Mitchell, "Family Time."

24. California Constitution, art. 16, sec. 20.

25. National Association of State Budget Officers, *Budget Processes in the States* (Washington, D.C.: National Association of State Budget Officers, 2008), 67–71.

26. California Budget Project, *Winners and Losers: Where Has the Money Gone?* (Sacramento: California Budget Project, January 2001); Burton Gordon Malkiel, *A Random Walk Down Wall Street: The Time-Tested Strategy for Successful Investing* (New York: W. W. Norton, 2003), 92; Michael Coleman, *VLF Facts: A Primer on the Motor Vehicle In-Lieu Tax, the Car Tax Cut and Backfill* (Davis, Calif.: Coleman Advisory Services, May 2006), http://www.californiaci-tyfinance.com/VLFfacts06.pdf.

27. Under SB 400, pensions for ordinary workers rose to 2 percent of their final twelve months' pay for each year of service when retiring at age 55, and to 2.5 percent at age 63; pensions for public safety workers went to 3 percent at age 50. Karon Green, "SB 400 Senate Bill—Bill Analysis," September 8, 1999, http://info.sen.ca.gov/pub/99–00/bill/sen/sb_0351–0400/sb_400_cfa_19990908 _063640_asm_floor.html.

28. Daniel Weintraub, "Cozy State Pension Deal Costs Taxpayers Billions," *Sacramento Bee*, August 10, 2003, F-1; Warren Buffett and Carol Lewis, "Mr. Buffett on the Stock Market," *Fortune*, November 22, 1999, http://money.cnn .com/magazines/fortune/fortune_archive/1999/11/22/269071/index.htm.

29. Committee for a Responsible Federal Budget, testimony of Maya Mac-Guineas on Renewing Statutory PAYGO, House Budget Committee, July 25, 2007, http://www.newamerica.net/publications/resources/2007/testimony_maya _macguineas_renewing_statutory_paygo; Richard Kogan, *The Need to Restore Pay-as-You-Go Budget Enforcement for Tax Cuts and Entitlements* (Washington, D.C.: Center on Budget and Policy Priorities, March 24, 2005), http://www .cbpp.org/cms/?fa=view&id=1216.

30. Katherine Barrett and Richard Greene, "Grading the States '08: A Management Report Card," in *Governing*, http://www.governing.com/gpp/2008/

index.htm; National Association of State Budget Officers, *Budget Processes in the States*, 40–47.

31. Dahl, *How Democratic Is the American Constitution?* 122.

6. THE ARCHITECTURE
OF POLITICAL FRUSTRATION

1. William T. Bagley, "Sacramento's Partisan Gridlock," *Marin Independent Journal*, February 6, 2008; see also "Restoring Confidence in the Legislative Process," Public Policy Institute of California, Sacramento, December 7, 2007, http://www.ppic.org/content/av/EventVideo_LegReformPanel_12_4_07.asf, for more vivid complaints by Pete Wilson, Willie Brown, and John Burton about the corrosive effects on legislative comity of a decline in drinking and lobbyist-funded "play," as well as, ironically, the open-meeting rules authored by Bagley himself.

2. Thad Kousser, "How Geopolitics Cleaved California's Republicans and United Its Democrats," *California Journal of Politics and Policy* 1, no. 1 (2009), http://www.bepress.com/cjpp/vol1/iss1/4; Lou Cannon, *Governor Reagan: His Rise to Power* (New York: PublicAffairs, 2003), 208–14.

3. Lisa McGirr, *Suburban Warriors: The Origins of the New American Right* (Princeton, N.J.: Princeton University Press, 2001); Pietro S. Nivola and David W. Brady, eds., *Red and Blue Nation*, vol. 1, *Characteristics and Causes of America's Polarized Politics* (Washington, D.C.: Brookings Institution and Hoover Institution, 2006).

4. Kousser, "How Geopolitics Cleaved California's Republicans," 3–6; Frédérick Douzet, "Residential Segregation and Political Balkanization," in Frédérick Douzet, Thad Kousser, and Kenneth P. Miller, eds., *The New Political Geography of California* (Berkeley, Calif.: Berkeley Public Policy Press, 2008), 45–70; Bill Bishop (with Richard Cushing), *The Big Sort: How the Clustering of the Like-Minded Is Tearing Us Apart* (New York: Mariner Books, 2009), 13, 173–217.

5. Robert Dahl, *How Democratic Is the American Constitution?* 2nd ed. (New Haven, Conn.: Yale University Press, 2003), 148.

6. Republicans Jim Nielsen and Dan Logue of AD 2 and AD 3 in the Sacramento Valley; Connie Conway of AD 34 in the southern San Joaquin Valley; Stephen Knight of AD 36 in desert high country; Curt Hagman of AD 60 in Orange County; Brian Nestande of AD 64 in Riverside; Jeff Miller in AD 71

straddling Orange and Riverside counties; Democrats Mariko Yamada of AD 8 in Yolo and Solano counties; Jerry Hill of AD 19 in San Mateo; Paul Fong of AD 22 in San Jose; Bob Blumenfeld of AD 40 in Los Angeles; John Pérez of AD 46 in Los Angeles; Isadore Hall of AD 52 in Los Angeles, Bonnie Lowenthal of AD 54 in Los Angeles; Norma Torres of AD 61 in San Bernardino.

7. Doolittle, who combined a choirboy demeanor with his bare-knuckles political style, was fined by the Fair Political Practices Commission but never looked back. His run did not end until he retired from the House of Representatives in 2008 after the FBI raided his home as part of an investigation of the Jack Abramoff lobbying scandal, in which Doolittle was later named by federal prosecutors as an unindicted co-conspirator.

8. John Stuart Mill, *Representative Government* (Charleston, S.C.: Forgotten Books, 2008), 87.

9. William H. Riker, "The Two-Party System and Duverger's Law: An Essay on the History of Political Science," *American Political Science Review* 76 (1982): 753–66.

10. Mark Baldassare et al., *PPIC Statewide Survey: Californians and Their Government* (San Francisco: Public Policy Institute of California, September 2008).

11. John Jacobs, *A Rage for Justice: The Passion and Politics of Phillip Burton* (Berkeley: University of California Press, 1995), 415.

12. J. Morgan Kousser, "Redistricting: 1971–2001," in Jerry Lubenow and Bruce E. Cain, eds., *Governing the Golden State: Politics, Government, and Public Policy in California* (Berkeley, Calif.: Institute of Governmental Studies Press, 1997), 137–55.

13. George Skelton, "Gerrymandering a Key Culprit in California Budget Mess," *Los Angeles Times*, August 28, 2008.

14. Eric McGhee, *Redistricting and Legislative Partisanship* (San Francisco: Public Policy Institute of California, 2008), 37, 72.

15. Alan I. Abramowitz, Brad Alexander, and Matthew Gunning, "Incumbency, Redistricting, and the Decline of Competition in U.S. House," *Journal of Politics* 68 (February 2006): 75–88; Mark Paul, "Redistricting Reform Draws a Map of Great Disappointment," *San Francisco Chronicle*, January 28, 2007, E-3.

16. Bruce E. Cain, Iris Hui, and Karin Mac Donald, "Sorting or Self-Sorting: Competition and Redistricting in California?" in Douzet, Kousser, and Miller, *New Political Geography*, 245–65.

17. Mark Paul, "Primary Gave Political Theorists a Reason to Smile," *Sacramento Bee*, June 8, 1998, B-5; Thad Kousser, "Crossing Over When It Counts: How the Motives of Voters in Blanket Primaries Are Revealed by Their Actions

in General Elections," in Bruce E. Cain and Elisabeth R. Gerber, eds., *Voting at the Political Fault Line: California's Experiment with the Blanket Primary* (Berkeley: University of California Press, 2002), 47–49.

18. *California Democratic Party et al. v. Jones, Secretary of State of California, et al.*, 530 U.S. 567 (2000), 577, 581–82.

19. We thank Micah Weinberg, our colleague at the New America Foundation, for data from his unpublished research on results of the 2008 Washington State primary.

20. *Washington State Grange v. Washington State Republican Party et al.*, 532 U.S. 06–713 (2008), http://www.law.cornell.edu/supct/html/06-713.ZS.html.

21. Our thanks to Eric McGhee of the Public Policy Institute of California for sharing his research on the primary rules and systems in use around the country; Elisabeth R. Gerber and Rebecca B. Morton, "Primary Election Systems and Representation," *Journal of Law, Economics, and Organization* 14 (1998): 304–24.

22. California Constitution, art. 16, sec. 2.5.

23. For a broader discussion of the constitutional principles behind making every vote count, see John R. Low-Beer, "The Constitutional Imperative of Proportional Representation," *Yale Law Journal* 94 (1984): 163–88.

7. REMAKING ELECTIONS AND THE LEGISLATURE

1. For a comparative analysis of democratic forms around the world, see Arend Lijphart, *Patterns of Democracy: Government Forms and Performance in Thirty-Six Countries* (New Haven, Conn.: Yale University Press, 1999).

2. Douglas J. Amy, *Real Choices/New Voices: How Proportional Representation Elections Could Revitalize American Democracy*, 2nd ed. (New York: Columbia University Press, 2002), 50–51.

3. The International Institute for Democracy and Electoral Assistance, an intergovernmental group promoting democracy around the world, tracks electoral systems on its Web site: http://www.idea.int/esd/world.cfm.

4. Various formulas are in use around the world to allocate seats in proportional representation elections. This example uses the d'Hondt formula, mathematically identical to the method originally devised by Thomas Jefferson to apportion seats in the House of Representatives among the states after each census. The d'Hondt formula allots each seat in a multimember district in succession by dividing each party's total vote by the sum of one plus the number of seats it has already won; the party with the highest quotient in the round wins

the seat. In this example, the Democrats get the first seat, the Republicans the second, the Democrats the third, Republicans the fourth, the Greens the fifth. Because different methods can yield somewhat different results—the d'Hondt formula, for example, tends to slightly favor the largest party—the choice of formula would be an important subject in designing a new electoral system. See Amy, *Real Choices/New Voices*, 259–62, for a description of the differences.

5. It is even possible to elect candidates from multimember districts in a way that takes parties out of the official equation altogether, using a ranked-choice voting system known in political science jargon as the single transferable vote (STV). Under this system, all the candidates get listed individually on the ballot and voters rank them. The winners are determined in a series of runoffs. But STV is not well suited for larger multimember districts. In districts with more than three seats, voters would have too many candidates to rank. For details on how the STV operates, see ibid., 263–66.

6. Illinois elected its State House of Representatives from three-member districts using a semiproportional system known as cumulative voting. Enraged at lawmakers for increasing their own pay during the economic turmoil of the late 1970s, voters there passed a measure known as the "cutback amendment," which reduced the membership of the legislature and created single-member districts. Many Illinois voters have come to regret their rash decision. The old system helped elect both Democrats and Republicans in most districts and opened the statehouse door to lawmakers at odds with Illinois's party machines but trusted by voters. Unhappy with the uncompetitive districts, polarization, leadership dominance, and corruption that have come with the change to single-member plurality elections, lawmakers in 2009 introduced legislation to return to the old system, and reformers began circulating petitions to place a "put back amendment" before the voters. Steven Hill, *10 Steps to Repair American Democracy* (Sausalito, Calif.: PoliPointPress, 2006), 63–71; Illinois Assembly on Political Representation and Alternative Electoral Systems, *Final Report and Recommendations* (Urbana-Champaign: University of Illinois, IGPA, 2001); Dan Carden, "Some Say Quinn's '79 Initiative Created Environment for Corruption," *Daily Herald*, May 19, 2009.

7. Matthew Soberg Shugart and Martin P. Wattenberg, "Introduction: The Electoral Reform of the Twenty-First Century?" in Matthew Soberg Shugart and Martin P. Wattenberg, eds., *Mixed-Member Electoral Systems: The Best of Both Worlds?* (Oxford: Oxford University Press, 2001), 1.

8. Matthew Soberg Shugart and Martin P. Wattenberg, "Mixed-Member

Electoral Systems: A Definition and Typology," in ibid., 9–24. For a detailed proposal to set up a regionalized mixed-member system in California, see Mark Paul and Micah Weinberg, "Remapping the California Electorate," in R. Jeffrey Lustig, ed., *Remaking California, Reclaiming the Public Good* (Berkeley, Calif.: Heyday Books, 2010). A similar proposal, which does not use regional elections, is offered by Kathleen Bawn in "Reforming Representation in California: Checks and Balances without Gridlock," in Bruce Cain and Roger Noll, eds., *Constitutional Reform in California* (Berkeley, Calif.: Institute of Governmental Studies Press, 1995), 129–59.

9. Sanford Levinson, *Our Undemocratic Constitution: Where the Constitution Goes Wrong (and How We the People Can Correct It)* (New York: Oxford University Press, 2006).

10. Alexander Hamilton, James Madison, and John Jay, *The Federalist: A Collection of Essays* (New York: Colonial Press, 1901), 305.

11. Ibid., 49.

12. The International Institute for Democracy and Electoral Assistance tracks the size of national legislatures on its Web site, http://www.idea.int/esd/world.cfm.

13. John Adams, quoted in Hanna Fenichel Pitkin, *The Concept of Representation* (Berkeley: University of California Press, 1972), 60.

14. California Constitution, art. 4, "Legislative," sec. 7.5.

15. California Constitution Revision Commission, *Final Report and Recommendations to the Governor and the Legislature* (Sacramento, 1996), 15–23.

16. "Educator Is Found Guilty of Conflict," *New York Times*, January 30, 1993, A-7.

17. Paul Jacobs, "Gray Davis' Political Pals Get Lucrative Posts," *Los Angeles Times*, October 17, 1993, A-1.

18. Virginia Ellis and Carl Ingram, "Quackenbush Resigns," *Los Angeles Times*, June 29, 2000, A-1.

19. Dan Morain, "Westly Joined Backer's Tax Fight," *Los Angeles Times*, May 27, 2006, A-1.

20. Christian Berthelsen, Vanessa Hua, and John Wildermuth, "Shelley Quits," *San Francisco Chronicle*, February 5, 2005, A-1.

21. See Dean Murphy, "New Runoff System in San Francisco Has the Rival Candidates Cooperating," *New York Times*, September 30, 2004, for an account of joint fund-raising and collaborative campaigning by rival candidates, a departure from the brawling and negative campaigning that was once the norm before San Francisco switched to IRV.

22. Chris Havens, "St. Paul Will Cast Vote on Instant-Runoff Elections," *Star Tribune*, October 18, 2009.

23. Francis Neely, Corey Cook, and Lisel Blash, *An Assessment of Ranked-Choice Voting in the San Francisco 2005 Election: Final Report* (San Francisco: San Francisco State University, Public Research Institute, 2006).

8. GOVERNMENT FROM THE BOTTOM UP

1. Carey McWilliams, *California: The Great Exception* (Berkeley: University of California Press, 1949), 8.

2. Population estimates and projections from the California Department of Finance, http://www.dof.ca.gov/research/demographic/reports/.

3. McWilliams, *California*, 20.

4. Ibid.

5. U.S. Census Bureau, *Demographic Trends in the 20th Century*, Census 2000 Special Reports, Series CENSR-4, http://www.census.gov/prod/2002pubs/censr-4.pdf.

6. Kevin Starr, *Americans and the California Dream*, 8 vols. (New York: Oxford University Press, 1973–2009).

7. McWilliams, *California*, 21.

8. Downsize California Web site, http://downsizeca.org; Bill Maze, interview with Craig Edwards, April 27, 2009, http://committedtoromney.com/?p=6590; Malia Wollan, "Farmers Lead a Bid to Create 2 Californias," *New York Times*, March 13, 2009, A9.

9. See Wollan, "Farmers Lead a Bid."

10. Frederick Rose, "Psycho-Economics: Can an Entire State Have an Identity Crisis?" *Wall Street Journal*, November 16, 1993, A-1; Peter Schrag, "Two States of California: An Undying Fantasy," *Sacramento Bee*, December 23, 2008, 19A; Bill McEwen, "Splitting the State Is a Sure Path to Poverty for the Valley," *Fresno Bee*, February 26, 2009, B-1.

11. Great Valley Center, *The State of the Great Valley of California: Assessing the Region via Indicators, the Economy* (Modesto, Calif.: Great Valley Center, October 2009), 8.

12. See Rose, "Psycho-Economics."

13. Legislative Analyst's Office (LAO), "Making Government Make Sense," *The 1993–94 Budget: Perspectives and Issues* (Sacramento, 1993), 111–30.

14. Peter Schaafsma, interview with the authors, November 12, 2009.

15. LAO, "Making Government Make Sense," 112.

16. Criminal justice outlays from reports by the state controller and legislative analyst; crime costs derived from estimates in Mark A. R. Kleiman, *When Brute Force Fails: How to Have Less Crime and Less Punishment* (Princeton, N.J.: Princeton University Press, 2009), 16–33.

17. Ibid., 91–92, 3.

18. LAO, "Making Government Make Sense," 122.

19. Kim Alexander, *California 2.0* (New America Foundation, June 24, 2009) video, http://www.youtube.com/watch?v = X1auuIQFFM.

20. LAO, "Making Government Make Sense," 125.

21. William B. Fulton, *The Reluctant Metropolis: The Politics of Urban Growth in Los Angeles* (Baltimore: Johns Hopkins University Press, 2001), 163–67; Monica Altmaier and others, *Make It Work: Implementing Senate Bill 375* (Berkeley: University of California, Berkeley, Institute of Urban and Regional Development, Center for a Sustainable California, 2009), 5–6.

22. California Constitution Revision Commission, *Final Report*, 71–77.

23. Schaafsma interview.

24. Heather R. McDonald and Stanton A. Glantz, "Political Realities of Statewide Smoking Legislation: The Passage of California's Assembly Bill 13," *Tobacco Control* 6 (1997): 41–54.

25. LAO, "Making Government Make Sense," 123–24.

9. A MORE DIRECT DEMOCRACY

1. Darrell Steinberg, interview with Joe Mathews for "California Can't Afford Propositions 1D and 1E," *Los Angeles Times*, April 23, 2009.

2. *Democracy by Initiative: Shaping California's Fourth Branch of Government*, 2nd ed. (Los Angeles: Center for Governmental Studies, 2008), 115–16.

3. Peter Hecht, "Field Poll: California Voters Oppose Five of Six May 19 Ballot Measures," *Sacramento Bee*, April 29, 2009, 1A.

4. Bruno Kaufmann, address to the First Global Forum on Modern Direct Democracy, Aarau, Switzerland, October 1, 2008.

5. *Democracy by Initiative*, 10; David Altman, address to the First Global Forum on Modern Direct Democracy, Aarau, Switzerland, October 1, 2008.

6. California Secretary of State records, including this list of referendums at http://www.sos.ca.gov/elections/referenda.htm.

7. Speaker's Commission on the California Initiative Process, *Final Report* (Sacramento, 2002); *Democracy by Initiative.*

8. *Democracy by Initiative*, 10, 115.

9. E. B. Willis and P. K. Stockton, *Debates and Proceedings of the Constitutional Convention*, vol. 1 (Sacramento: State Printing Office, 1880), 150–51.

EPILOGUE.
GOOD RULES TO MATCH ITS MOUNTAINS

1. Pew Center on the States, *Beyond California: States in Fiscal Peril* (Washington, D.C.: November 2009), 1.

2. Ibid., 5–6.

3. Paul Krugman, "Paranoia Strikes Deep," *New York Times*, November 9, 2009.

4. C. Wright Mills, *The Causes of World War III* (New York: M. E. Sharpe, 1985), 86.

5. Carey McWilliams, *California: The Great Exception* (Berkeley: University of California Press, 1949), 367.

6. William Butler Yeats, "Leda and the Swan." The full stanza in the poem from which McWilliams quoted is:

> The broken wall, the burning roof and tower
> And Agamemnon dead.
> Being so caught up,
> So mastered by the brute blood of the air,
> Did she put on his knowledge with his power
> Before the indifferent beak could let her drop?

The burning tower, broken wall, and Agamemnon all refer to the disastrous Greek war with Troy, and the "she" of the final stanzas is Leda, a mortal woman who crossed boundaries by having sex with Zeus, king of the gods, and triggered so much misery. The question the poem seems to ask is one that might be asked of California. Is it smart to follow your heart and instincts, damn the long-term consequences?

ACKNOWLEDGMENTS

All books are collaborations, even those that do not, like this one, get written with four hands on the keyboard or lean so heavily on the experience and insight of others. The graciousness and generosity that others extended to us, and to the idea of this book, stripped enough layers off our pessimism about California's future that it will take several quarts of disappointment to fully restore it.

This book draws heavily on interviews we have conducted over two careers in California journalism, between us spanning three decades, in which we have had the fortune to draw on the insights of hundreds of players in the state's political and policy fights, their names too numerous to individually thank here. But we wish to acknowledge in particular those who gave their time as we were writing the book, many of whom are directly quoted in it: Phil Angelides, Debra Bowen, Jim Brulte, Tim Gage, Gary Hart, Bill Hauck, Tim Hodson, Phil Isenberg, Gale Kaufman, Thad Kousser, Clarence Lo, Bill Lockyer, Sandy Muir, Dowell Myers, Peter Schaafsma, Arnold Schwarzenegger, Darrell Steinberg, and Jim Wunderman.

Many of the ideas we offer in the book got road tested and tuned up, in print and at conferences, by editors and fellow panelists. Sue Horton, Susan Brenneman, Tina Brown, Edward Felsenthal, Joel Fox, Chandra Sharma, Mark Schmitt, Harold Meyerson, John Pomfret, David Patterson, Ivan Oransky, Greg Veis, Kate Marsh, Adam Garfinkel, Gary Spiecker, Anthony York, John Howard, Jerry Roberts, Phil Trounstine, Howard Weaver, Bill Moore, Stuart Leavenworth, and Gary Reid gave us chances to try out early versions of the material and helped steer us in good directions. Bob Stern, Anthony Rubenstein, Rick Jacobs, Michael Coleman, Camden McEfee, Bill Deverell, Kirk Stark, Darien Shanske, David Gamage, Steve Chessin, Jim Mayer, Fred Silva, Zabrae Valentine, Vikram Amar, Lenny Goldberg, Kate Karpilow, Frank Mecca, James Harrison, Steve Churchwell, John Grubb, Michael Feinstein, Nancy Jamison, Ellen Hanak, Paul Rosenstiel, Stuart Drown, Whitney Barazoto, Russell Hancock, Wendy Nussbaum, PJ Mark, Loren Kaye, Jon Fleischman, John Chiang, David Crane, Lenny Mendonca, Tom Steyer, and Noel Perry offered platforms on which to speak or the benefit of their responses to what we had to say—and sometimes both. We owe special thanks to Gregory Rodriguez, Laura Villalpando, Swati Pandey, and Dulce Vasquez of Zócalo Public Square, a California treasure dedicated to building an audience for the state's best ideas and art; and to Gary Dymski, A. G. Block, Kelly Bradfield, and Andrew Crotto of the University of California Center Sacramento, another California treasure that connected the world of ideas to the world of state politics—a treasure dismantled by the university's shortsighted administration at the end of 2009.

The New America Foundation has afforded us what every writer needs: support to follow the evidence where it leads, no matter whose political interests were gored, and colleagues eager to both debate and help. Steve Coll read the manuscript, asked probing questions, and gave encouragement. Rachel White, Simone Frank, Danielle Maxwell, and Troy Schneider kept the lights on, the money flowing, the servers humming, and the Web sites fresh. Leif Wellington Haase, director of the California program, read the manuscript and became this project's top cheerleader. Micah Weinberg and Mark Paul co-authored an earlier version of the mixed-member electoral proposal in Chapter 7; he was a valuable sounding board for our ideas, both as we developed them and after we converted them to electrons. With their own work and ideas, Steven Hill, Blair Bobier, and Gauttam Dutta of the political reform program pointed us in bold and useful directions, though they bear no blame for where we have taken them. Our other California colleagues—Gregory Rodriguez, T. A. Frank, Rick Wartzman, Olivia Calderon, Anne Stuhldreher, Camille Esch, Lisa Margonelli, Doug McGray, Tomás Jiménez, Annette Nellen, Elizabeth Wu, Hosai Eshan, Claudie Bustamante, and Maria Sotero—were a constant source of ideas, support, and friendship. The James Irvine Foundation provided much of the funding that has made possible their work and ours.

Jack Citrin, Ethan Rarick, and Liz Weiner provided a comfortable second home for Mark Paul as a visiting scholar at the Institute of Governmental Studies at UC Berkeley. IGS's resources have been invaluable, and its contribution to Californians' knowledge about their politics and government, under Citrin's leadership and that of his predecessors, Bruce Cain and the late Nelson Polsby, is without peer.

Many colleagues in journalism, some now lured or driven to other endeavors, have been both friends and valued teachers about things California: Daniel Weintraub, Evan Halper, Peter Nicholas, Bob Salladay, Mitchell Benson, Rhea Wilson, Susanna Cooper, Ginger Rutland, Tom Philp, Jim Richardson, Susan Rasky, and the late John Jacobs. The same is true on the policy front. Juan Fernandez, Barbara Lloyd, Ted Eliopoulos, Anne Stausboll, Peter Taylor, Dan Dowell, John Hiber, Jim Zerio, Robert Feyer, Dan Feitelberg, and Nathan Brostrom were our guides to the world of public finance and pensions. Jean Ross, Elizabeth Hill, H. D. Palmer, Mike Genest, Chris Woods, John Griffing, Martin Helmke, Brad Williams, Daniel Mitchell, Edward Leamer, and Steven Levy provided us with a world-class education in fiscal policy and its relation to the economy. This book would not have been possible without the work and generosity of the scholars at the Public Policy Institute of California. We are especially indebted to Mark Baldassare for his probing of California public opinion; Eric McGhee for sharing his data on primary elections; Jed Kolko for his research on regional economics and business location decisions; and Max Neiman for conducting a rolling seminar on the relationship between state and local governments.

In addition to our New America colleagues and editors mentioned above, Bruno Kaufmann, Jonathan Marshall, Rick Jacobs, Peter Schrag, and two anonymous reviewers read all or part of the manuscript. They saved us from several mistakes and a few episodes of tone-deafness, and they pushed us to rethink or strengthen some of our arguments, for which we are grateful. Any remaining mistakes and infelicities are the fault of our own pigheadedness.

This book looks to the future, but writing it depended on access to the past. We are indebted to archivists and librarians around California—to the UC Hastings College of Law and its indispensable database on a century of California initiatives; Linda Johnson and the entire staff at the State Archives; David Kessler and the staff at the Bancroft Library; and the staffs of the Los Angeles County Law Library, the Witkin State Law Library, the UC Berkeley libraries, and the California State Library. The results of our research in those libraries could not have made it so quickly into print without the thinking and writing tools created by two practitioners of handcrafted software: Mark Bernstein, the developer of Tinderbox, and Keith Blount, the developer of Scrivener.

At the University of California Press, our editor, Kim Robinson, was quick to see the value of this project, forceful in championing it for a quick turnaround, and helpful in shaping the final manuscript. Janet Mowery, our copyeditor, saved us from some badly turned phrases and muddy explanations. David Peattie and his colleagues at BookMatters were supportive and efficient in moving the manuscript through production.

Writing a book can be all-consuming for the authors, but it at least comes with offsetting satisfactions—the joy of discovery, the exhilaration of a phrase finally wrestled into English, the sense of purpose. For an author's family, there are no offsets. They see only the backs of heads as we turn for days on end to the computer. They hear only the crankiness. To our wives, Robin Netzer and Anna Wilde Mathews, and to our sons, Jonah, Aaron, and Ben, we owe thanks for putting up with us through the manic months and helping us through them with grace and generosity. This book is as much their work as ours.

INDEX

Text:	11/15 Granjon
Display:	Akzidenz Grotesk
Compositor:	BookMatters, Berkeley
Printer and binder:	Maple-Vail Book Manufacturing Group